BUDOJI

A TALE OF THE DIVINE CITY OF ANCIENT KOREA

with an overview of Korean Shamanism

original text by Jesang Park
commentary & analysis by Sungje Cho
translation & edit by Seo Choi

Alpha Sisters Publishing, LLC
5174 McGinnis Ferry Road #348
Alpharetta, GA 30005
alphasisterspublishing.com

Original Text by Jesang Park
Plain Translation, Interpretation, Appendix in Korean by Sungje Cho
English Translation and Editing by Seo Choi

Illustrator: Meesha Goldberg
Editor: E. Ce Miller
Publisher: Seo Choi
Book Designer: Sheenah Freitas
Translation Support: Julie Moon, Minju Park

Library of Congress Cataloging-in-Publication Data is available upon request.

First Edition
ISBN 979-8-9869373-0-4 (paperback)
ISBN 979-8-9869373-1-1 (e-book)

Printed in the United States of America

To Our Ancestors

Table *of* Contents

BUDOJI

ILLUSTRATIONS
97

APPENDICES

THE CREATIVE TEAM
175

Introduction

Budoji (부도지) was written by Park Jesang (363 – 419 CE), a loyal official of the Silla Kingdom of ancient Korea. It contains the culture and early beliefs of Korea's earliest ancestors from 2333 BCE, including stories about the creation of the world as well as the origins, evolution, and migratory movements of the Korean people.

Budo refers to both a nation that acts in accordance with the Divine and to a capital city. Thus, in the name Budo, the will of Heaven is fulfilled on Earth. This is the founding principle on which Ancient Joseon (GoJoseon, 고조선), the kingdom of Dangun (단군), was built. Yet, over time, this once-existent kingdom has been relegated to myth.

Interest in *Budoji* has grown in recent years, and several people have attempted to translate the ancient text. However, the profound philosophy in the original document has yet to be fully captured. While the same may also be said about this text, I believe that providing a deeper analysis and explanation of *Budoji* requires understanding Korean Shamanism. In the spirit of that understanding, I have interpreted *Budoji* through the lens of Korean Shamanism while staying true to the original document.

Since ancient times, humans have felt a sense of awe and reverence toward supernatural powers. In the era *Budoji* describes, this was expressed in the worship of the sky through offerings and rituals called *jesa* (제사). Those who led these rituals, the chief priests, were also the tribal rulers of the period. Because these priests led their people based on divine revelations from Heaven, their divinity was regarded as both a kind of sorcery and the most advanced science of the time.

This divinity, *Chunbu* (천부), has been retained in the practices and rituals of Korean shamans (*mudang*, 무당) today. As just one example, archaeological finds from the Ancient Joseon period—in particular, a bronze mirror, sword, and rattle—are still used as the main tools of modern Korean shamans. In this way, Shamanic culture preserved many of the divine practices of ancient times, allowing contemporary Korean Shamanism to act as a window to the era of *Budoji*.

There are claims that *Budoji*, which conveys the great creation myth of the Korean people, is a fake document with fictitious myths with little historical or cultural significance. This is an erroneous perception made by those who wrongly assume that *Budoji* is intended to be read only as history. While the existence of Ancient Joseon has been verified as a historical fact, many still regard it as myth. Similarly, there are those who deny the true nature of Dangun's Ancient Joseon as it appears in *Budoji*, considering the text little more than a collection of folktales. But just as Greek, Roman, Nordic, and Chinese mythologies are commonly studied to understand ancient life, *Budoji* offers a yet-untapped treasure trove of the great philosophies of early Koreans.

Since the beginning of time, humans have developed means of recording the traditions and rituals of societies, as well as the great changes that have taken place throughout the rise and fall of civilizations. But it is only in relatively recent history that these records were captured via writing systems. For most of human history, information was recorded not in writing but passed down through oral traditions. It can thus be inferred that myths are accounts of civilizations that existed before the written word—stories of ancient kingdoms that were spoken from one generation to the next, though perhaps never preserved through text. This, however, makes them no less true.

One of the primary ways oral traditions get lost in history is through their strategic destruction by colonizing empires. In Korea, during the Japanese Colonial Period, Imperial Japan made great efforts to reconstruct Korean history to fit the Japanese worldview and narrative interests. In this process, the existence of Ancient Joseon was relegated to myth. This distorted and incorrect interpretation of Korean history created during the Japanese Colonial Era prevails today and is still being blindly believed and taught by positivist historians in Korea. However, in an effort to restore some of the ancient Korean wisdom that has been lost or deliberately silenced over time, I encourage more people to read and share the story of *Budoji*.

Moving forward, I hope that many scholars from both the East and the West find interest in *Budoji* and contribute to the research that reveals the beginnings and migratory movements of early Koreans.

— Sungje Cho

Publisher's Note

I grew up in South Korea in the seventies and eighties. As a strong-willed girl, the world influenced by Confucian values and patriarchy seemed determined to hold me inside a box designed to keep me small, quiet, and submissive.

When I immigrated to the United States in the nineties, I thought I was escaping to the land of freedom: liberation. I was eager to assimilate, thinking that the sooner I adapted to mainstream "American" ways and rejected the "foreignness" of my Korean ancestry, the better my life would be.

After over 30 years of living that way, I realized I had been rejecting and distancing myself from who I truly was—how I had been participating in and normalizing the problematic system of white-washing my identity to fit in or be accepted. I wanted to change that; I wanted to embrace my Korean roots and culture again, to truly be a proud Korean American.

Yet what I perceived as "traditionally Korean" still felt oppressive. Most of the traditions I considered returning to were rooted in patriarchal values, with hints of misogyny, classism, and gross inequality. How could I, a strong woman of color wanting to fight inequality and racism in this land I now call home, embrace values and beliefs from my motherland that also felt oppressive and unjust?

This led me to question and research the ancient Korean wisdom that originated many thousands of years before the birth of Confucius and the subsequent Confucian influence on Korea's culture during and after the Joseon Dynasty.

Today, much of what is seen and read in the West about ancient Korean culture is from the Joseon Dynasty (1392–1897 CE), Korea's most recent, pre-modernization kingdom. Foreign, non-indigenous beliefs, like Buddhism and Confucianism, heavily influenced much of the "traditional Korean values" we see today. Discovering this, I started to wonder what indigenous Korean culture was like thousands of years before the adoption of these foreign beliefs.

What was my motherland really like in her beginning?

My search to find the indigenous wisdom of my ancestors, along with my personal spiritual awakening, led me to the books of author Sungje Cho. When we met in person in 2018 to discuss his books on Korean Shamanism, he casually mentioned *Budoji* and its stories. I was astounded to hear of the existence of an ancient book, written thousands of years ago, filled with tales about a time even thousands of years earlier—a Korean origin story about the creation of the universe, the dawn of humanity, and more!

Reading *Budoji* was one of the most powerful experiences of my search into the indigenous wisdom of Korea. It felt like a missing piece—repairing disconnections, filling that empty space I felt within myself about being Korean. The beliefs and values I'd always imagined my Korean ancestors held dissolved. I finally discovered a deep connection to the wisdom of my ancestors. I no longer felt oppressed and unseen, but rather empowered and represented.

I learned that my ancestors—our ancestors—believed that the entire universe blossomed from a universal vibration, a sound wave, an energy called *YulYeo*. They believed that a goddess named Mago and her two daughters, the embodiment of the divine feminine, worked with this vibrational energy to create every living thing on earth, including humans. Hello, feminine power!

Ancient Korean ancestors believed in living in harmony with the Divine, nature, and other humans. They honored the heavens (the sky) as a representation of the Divine, the land (nature) as representing all of the earth, and prioritized living in harmony and with equality. This indigenous wisdom tradition opposed oppression, colonization and conquest, and centralized power designed to control other humans.

My ancestors believed in fostering a deep connection to the spiritual by performing rituals and ceremonies. Yet central to their faith in the Divine was the practice of living in harmony with the land and all the human community. Ancient Korean Shamanism never sought to become a dogmatic establishment with a rigid doctrine designed to be used by a select few in establishing power and control over others. It was always an indigenous wisdom tradition, accessible to everyone and incorporated into the routines and rituals of daily life and passed down, generation to generation.

I am so proud to introduce the first English translation and publication of *Budoji*. My hope is that readers from the Korean diaspora feel the same deep soul connection to this text that I did and find their own healing within the stories of our earliest ancestors. My wish is that all who read this find empowerment within the indigenous wisdom and feel encouraged to seek harmony with the Divine, nature, and all the human and more-than-human beings we share our world with.

With this book, may you pause, inquire, and connect.

— *Seo Choi*

BUDOJI

Original Text
with Interpretation

CHAPTER 1

Mago's Land & the Birth of Mago Samshin

Magosung¹ is the highest place on earth.
It succeeded the heavenly realm in accordance with
  Divine Ways.²

Four heavenly people built structures in each of the four corners
  and made sounds.

The first was Hwang-Gung, the second was Baek-So, the third was
  Chung-Gung, and the fourth was Heuk-So.

Gung-hee was the mother of two Gungs, and So-hee was the mother of two Sos.
They were both the daughters of Mago.

Mago was born out of Jimse³ and had no human emotions, so she mated with the

---

1) *Mago's land.* In English, the Korean *sung* translates to *castle* or *fortress*, but when describing the pre-kingdom mythic period, this translation will use *Magosung* to mean *Mago's land* or *Mago's paradise.*

2) Also, *Chunbu.* The Divine Ways or symbols representing the divinity.

3) The period from birth to extinction. It is believed each *Jimse* signifies one cycle of birth to extinction.

sky to give birth to two daughters without a spouse.

Gung-hee and So-hee also received seed from the sky to give birth to two heavenly sons and two heavenly daughters without marriage.

In total, there were four heavenly men and four heavenly women.

INTERPRETATION

Mago (마고) is the ultimate creation goddess credited with creating the earth and humanity. *Ma* means *mother* or *goddess,* and *Go* means *origin* or *old.* In other words, Mago is the mother of origin, the mother of Earth and all things on it, the goddess of the creation of the universe. At *Magosung* (마고성), Samshin (삼신)[4] began with Mago and two daughters—the divine goddesses Gung-hee and So-hee. All three were capable of parthenogenesis (asexual reproduction) and gave birth to the four heavenly clans.

Hwang-Gung (황궁) was a yellow-skinned clan that managed the earth element in *Magosung.* Their descendants are believed to have lived around what is present-day Korea, Japan, northern China, Manchuria, and Siberia. The Hwang-Gung clan is the origin of the Korean people.

Baek-So (백소) was a white-skinned clan that managed the air element. Their descendants are believed to have lived around what is present-day Europe. Heuk-So (흑소) was a black-skinned clan that managed the fire element. Their descendants are believed to have lived around what is present-day Africa and the Middle East. Chung-Gung (청궁) was a blue-skinned clan that managed the water element. Their descendants are believed to have disappeared, but stories and examples of blue-skinned people living in ancient times have been retained, including records of blue-skinned costumes and masks of the Mayan and Aztec people.

As Mago and her two daughters form the ultimate god of Samshin (also called Mago Samshin), many areas in modern Korea are named

---

4) Three Spirit, Triple Goddess.

after Mago in various local dialects. Mt. Jirisan has a *Nogodan* altar and a history of Mago mythology. Jeju Island recognizes the myth of Yungdeung Halmi Baram, Gyeongbuk Province is home to Mt. Magosan, and the town of Gochang features Mt. Bangjangsan.

There is also a record of Mago in *Goryeosa (History of Goryeo)* (918–1392 CE) in Volume 36 of the King Chunghae section. There is a phrase that reads "as the descendants of Mago," indicating the people of the Goryeo Dynasty[5] still called themselves *Magojina*—"Mago's country."

Nogodan, an altar dedicated to Mago on Mt. Jirisan, built during the Silla Kingdom

Image source: Seo Choi

---

5) See Appendix 3 for the list of Korean ancient kingdom eras.

CHAPTER 2
Creation

In the beginning, Magosung was above Sildalsung,[6]
  next to Huhdalsung.[7]
The only light and warmth came from the sun, and nothing
  yet had shape.
Eight notes of sound could be heard from the sky.

Both Sildalsung and Huhdalsung came from this sound and
Magosung and Mago herself came from it too.
This was Jimse.
Before Jimse, YulYeo[8] repeated itself several times to create the stars.

Toward the end of Jimse, Mago birthed Gung-hee and So-hee
and let them manage Oeum-Chiljo.[9]
Finally, Earth Milk rose from the center of the land.

---

6) Pre-formed earth, or planet.

7) The moon.

8) Eight notes of sound, the divine energetic force or vibration that created the universe.

9) Five notes and seven keys, the high/low and long/short echo of *YulYeo*.

*The Hees gave birth to four heavenly men and four heavenly women
and raised them by feeding them Earth Milk,
The four heavenly women controlled Yeo, and the four heavenly men
    controlled Yul.*

INTERPRETATION

This chapter explains the beginning of the universe and the creation
of humanity.

First, there was only sunlight and eight sound notes without any
physical form. This suggests similarities between the Big Bang and the
Chaos. *Sildalsung* (실달성) is the unformed earth—the planet before it
took the shape of Earth as we know it. *Huhdalsung* (허달성) is the moon.

In the first chapter of Lao Tzu's *Tao Te Ching*, he mentions, "The
nameless is the beginning of the universe and having the name is the
mother of all things."

In ancient Asian philosophy, the Earth's energy was thought to
be divided into eight directions. This coincides with *YulYeo* (율여), the
eight notes of sound. *YulYeo*, through its force and vibration, created the
universe. It also represents the earth's energy vibrating, with light and
sound, to take its current form.

In *Samsung-gi*, the ancient text of Ancient Joseon, it was written,
"One divine person in Siberia became the sole god that transformed from
the sky, the bright light hit the entire universe, and the big interaction
created all things."

Jimse (짐세) refers to a period of birth to extinction, each *Jimse*
indicating one cycle. The Jurassic geologic period is one example of *Jimse*,
while as human beings, we live during another. With the existence of
Mago, the *Jimse* of humans began.

Gung-hee and So-hee gave birth to the heavenly sons and daughters and let them manage the *Oeum-Chiljo* (오음칠조)—the five notes and
seven keys, the variations of *YulYeo*. If *YulYeo* was the sound of heaven

creating the universe, *Oeum-Chiljo* could be considered the sound of the creation of life in the universe. It can be said that all living things on Earth were born through the sounds of the *Oeum-Chiljo*.

Earth Milk was the sustenance or energy source that fed the heavenly men, women, and their descendants living in Mago's land. As the earth provided a divine food source for humans, people did not need to eat anything else.

The four heavenly women oversaw *Yeo*, controlling the high and low pitch through feminine Yin vibrations. The four heavenly men were in charge of *Yul*, managing the long and short echoes through the masculine Yang vibrations. These four divine couples were in charge of giving birth to all living beings on the earth.

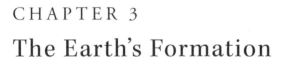

CHAPTER 3
The Earth's Formation

Once Huchun began operating and YulYeo recon-
    structed itself,
Harmony was made, and there was balance.

Mago pulled the Sildalsung down into the heavenly water
and its energy rose up to form water clouds.

Then Sildalsung opened up wide, creating land in the middle.
The ocean and land aligned side by side
and the mountains and streams stretched wide.

The Earth started rotating and shifting, creating waves.
Air, fire, water, and earth began mixing and harmonizing.
The sun created day and night, and four seasons formed,
raising plants and the beasts of the earth to abundance.

There was more work to be done on all the land.
So the four heavenly pairs divided up and managed the original sounds.

Hwang managed earth, Chung managed water,
Baek managed air, and Heuk managed fire.

Each built a camp in which to perform their duties, and these later became
  four clans.

Air and fire worked together; there was no darkness or coldness in the sky.
Water and earth worked together; the ground had no deformity or ugliness.
This was so the sound vibrated, giving light from above and harmony from below.

INTERPRETATION

Huchun (후천) translates to *later heaven* and signifies the world that came after Mago's appearance, with all her creations. The period before Mago's arrival was *Sunchun* (선천), or *before heaven*, signifying the world before the current formation of the universe.

Sildalsung was considered Earth before it became the Earth we now know. Mago lifted it and dropped it into the pool of heavenly water, causing it to split open and create the land, the sea, the mountains, and the rivers.

Mago initiated a series of significant vibrational changes to continue creating all the other elements of Earth, including night, day, and the four seasons. This process also began the Earth's rotation and other energetic forces. Finally, Earth became a place to sustain plants and animals, and the heavenly people managed all these activities. They were each represented by a color—yellow, blue, white, or black—and managed the four elements of nature—earth, water, air, or fire. They later became four clans and worked harmoniously.

CHAPTER 4
The Creation of Humans

While eight heavenly people managed the origi-
   nal sounds,
there wasn't any responsibility for the continuation of the
   sound notes.
Everything appeared in one moment and disappeared in the next,
   which was difficult to control.

Finally, Mago ordered the four heavenly men and four heavenly women
   to open their sides and procreate. They married one another and gave
   birth to three sons and three daughters.
This was the origin of human beings on Earth.

The men and women continued procreating over several generations
and the number of humans in Magosung increased to three thousand per clan.

From this point on, the twelve pairs of original humans guarded the gates,
while their descendants divided up the task of the continued operation of the
   sound notes.
Finally, the life force and flow of Earth achieved balance.

Every person in Mago's land was pure in character, intuitively knowing how to live
    in harmony with all.
Because they only drank Earth Milk for sustenance, their blood and souls were
    clear and bright. Their ears had Ogeum,[10] *enabling them to hear the sounds*
    from heaven wholly,
and they could not only walk and run but also take off and fly to travel freely
    across distances.

Once their life mission was completed, their bodies turned into gold dust.
Yet their spirit bodies remained on Earth.
They knew how to communicate without sound and move around without
    being seen.
The spirit bodies lived forever, spread alongside the energy of Earth.

INTERPRETATION

YulYeo are the original sounds of creation, comprised of *Oeum-Chiljo*, the variations of five notes and seven keys which, together, make up *YulYeo*. While eight heavenly people tried managing the original sounds maintaining Earth, there was more work to be done running and operating the various vibrations of all living things—tending the high and low, long and short, and the echoes. This means while the creation of all things was happening, the continuation of the life force was inconsistent. Some did not live long after being born, and others did not thrive.

Therefore, Mago ordered the eight heavenly people to create more humans. From then on, humans gave birth to offspring through intercourse between man and woman, evolving humanity from parthenogenesis into the era of sexual reproduction.

Then, the four heavenly couples each birthed three sons and three daughters, producing twelve men and twelve women and, therefore,

---

10) An oratory organ, or function of the human ear, believed at the time to enable humans to hear *YulYeo*, the divine sounds or the sound of the heavens.

twelve couples. These twelve pairs were the origin of all subsequent humans on Earth. Eventually, the population increased to 3000 per clan. In the ancient texts of *Handangogi* and *Samguk Yusa*, there are mentions of Hwan-Ung (환웅) descending to the Mt. Taebeaksan with three thousand people.

So, the twelve pairs of heavenly humans took charge of *YulYeo*, breathing life into all creation, and their descendants perpetuated harmony by managing and nurturing the lives of all beings. In this way, the number twelve came to mean something significant in the cycle of human life: the twelve months of the year, for example.

All humans in Mago's land were pure and bright in nature and understood the Divine Ways of creating and nurturing the Earth. Their wisdom and character came from the Earth Milk, giving them clarity in blood and spirit. The *Ogeum* (오금) afforded them the specific ability to hear the sounds and notes from the sky. Listening to heaven and earth contributed to the clarity and brightness of their spirits.

Humans in those times could not only walk and run but also jump to travel great distances quickly, suggesting some superhuman physical abilities. This ability to travel at speed, as if flying, has been written of in many ancient Asian stories of deities, martial artists, and saints.

They also did not fear death. Once their lives ended, their bodies turned to gold dust or precious metals. At the same time, their souls continued to live on earth—communicating freely without sound and traveling freely without being seen, enabling their eternal lives as a part of the Earth.

CHAPTER 5
Omi Incident

A man named Jiso in the Baek-So clan went to the well
   to drink Earth Milk.
There were many people, and the well was small.
He did not drink, instead giving way to many people
   ahead of him.
This repeated five times.

He returned home, and he fell from hunger.
A faint sound rang in his ears, drawing his attention to grapes on a vine.
He tasted the grapes and experienced Omi.[11]

As he ate the grapes, he stood up and jumped up and down, feeling the power of
   the grapes.
He left home and began marching and singing.

"Heaven and earth are wide and big! Yet my own power surpasses them.
How can this be the power of the Divine? It is the power of grapes."

People doubted Jiso's words, but he convinced them they were true.

---

11) The five flavors: sweet, sour, bitter, salty, and spicy.

*People got curious and tried eating the grapes, then realized his words to be true.
Many in each clan ate the grapes.*

INTERPRETATION

This chapter introduces the *Omi* Incident (오미의 난), the turning point in
this human creation myth: what happened with the population increase
and the perceived idea of limited resources.

When Jiso returned hungry, after not drinking the Earth Milk—the
divine sustenance—he heard the seductive sound of grapes rather than
the heavenly sound of *YulYeo*. When he followed the sound and ate the
grapes, he was shocked by the temporary power of the grapes.

Perhaps grapes represent the forbidden fruit only reserved for gods,
similar to a metaphor like the apple of Eden in the Christian Bible. In fact,
the area east of Tibet near the Pamir mountains is an area called Turpan,
famous for producing grapes and raisins. In the Old Testament Genesis 9,
there is a story depicting Noah farming grapes and becoming drunk from
too much wine. Both Noah and Jiso lost their way through grapes.

Then Jiso ascends from his camp, marching and singing. This
"song" of sound became the first attempt by humans to imitate the
YulYeo sounds.

This *Omi* Incident is a turning point in the human history of Mago's
land.

People who used to be sustained by Earth Milk could hear the heavenly sounds and maintain their clear spirit, not succumbing to human
emotions but remaining calm and at peace. But after eating another
living thing, Jiso experienced a significant change in his body.

First, he was mesmerized by the flavor. After tasting grapes, his
taste buds opened to *Omi*, the five flavors of bitter, sweet, salty, sour, and
spicy. Humans first experiencing these five flavors signified they also
began experiencing *Chiljung*—the seven human emotions discussed in
Confucianism: happiness, anger, sadness, fear, love, hatred, and desire.

By drinking Earth Milk, humans could maintain their connection to divinity; but with the first eating of grapes—discovering flavors and emotions—humanity became corrupted. Some of the natural side effects of human emotion are that they can lead to conflict and antagonism. This *Omi* Incident marks the beginning of the human experience of feelings and emotion-motivated action—experiences like love, comradery, envy, spite, greed, and even hatred of humans and other living beings. This ended the peacefulness of *Magosung*.

The *Omi* Incident marks where humans broke from their divine existence and evolved toward becoming more like humans as we know them today—the humanity that has led to our history of wars, colonization, and other sufferings.

CHAPTER 6

The Disastrous Effects of the *Omi* Incident

When the people of the Baek-So clan first realized this,
    they were astonished.
They began to monitor and ban the consumption of grapes,
which destroyed people's ability to rely on their own
    self-restraint.

Once eating fruit was prohibited,
Mago closed the gates and removed the protective screen over the land.
The people who became in the habit of eating fruit all grew teeth,
and their saliva became poisonous, like that of snakes—
all because they forcefully consumed another living thing.

The people who did the work of monitoring the bans placed upon others
    grew eyes that brightened like those of an owl—all because they regarded the
    heavenly sounds carelessly.

In this way, the people's blood and flesh became murky.
Their hearts became so hardened that they finally lost their divine nature.
The Ogeum in their ears crumbled into dust
and the people could no longer hear the heavenly sounds.

Human feet grew heavy, and the ground beneath them became hard—
they no longer could take off and fly.
Their souls became so impure that many people were born with features
*   like animals.*

Their lives became shorter, and they no longer transitioned at death,
they instead became rot—all because their souls got confused by doubt
*   and shrunk.*

INTERPRETATION

When the people of *Magosung* began to eat other living beings, they destroyed the natural divine balance and changed people's physical and spiritual bodies. Human life became entangled with human desires and emotions, and their divine souls shrunk from doubt and mistrust.

CHAPTER 7
The First Punishment of Humans

*Since people were casting blame and bitterness, Jiso felt
   great shame.*
*He took his family and descendants and left the Magosung
   and went far away and hid.*

*The people who ate the grapes and the people who were prohibiting
   them also left, scattering from place to place.*

Hwang-Gung pitied them and said to them at parting:

"You've had so much doubt and mistrust that
your faces and natures have mutated,
and we cannot live together on the land.
But if you work hard to return yourselves to your true nature
and cleanse away the doubt and insidiousness,
you will be able to return to the beginning.
Please try and try again."

In time, the air and earth grew misaligned, and the land became dark and cold.
*Water and fire lost their harmony, and all beings with blood became envious
   and greedy.*

Mago had removed its protective screen over the Earth
so heavenly light could no longer reflect,
and had closed the gates so people could no longer hear the sound from the sky.

INTERPRETATION

In realizing all the side effects of the *Omi* Incident—the eating of the grapes—people began blaming Jiso, feeling hatred towards him. This demonstrates that the seven human emotions started affecting even those who had not eaten the grapes. While Jiso never could have anticipated such a curse would befall his people by his first consumption of grapes, he felt responsible for all that followed and decided to leave. Jiso's departure marked the first instance in which humans split from living as a single communal unit, going their separate ways for the first time—the first punishment since the *Omi* Incident.

Hwang-Gung was saddened, yet encouraged the humans to make efforts to change their beings back to their original true nature.[12] He suggested that, in doing so, they would be able to return to the paradise of *Magosung*.

However, the land of Mago was no longer a comfortable place, even for those who stayed. The elements of air and earth clashed instead of remaining in alignment, hindering the earth's rotation around the sun, and causing the seasons to disappear. The world became dark and cold. The elements of water and fire fell out of balance, changing the environment to force every living being—each human and every animal—into a competition for survival.

The true nature Hwang-Gung refers to is *Sun Chung Hu* (선청후): a good, clear, and generous mind. The trifecta of Goodness, Clearness, and Generosity was the core foundation upon which humanity came into being as a part of nature and the universe—the principle of Samshin philosophy.[13] It is this nature that Hwang-Gung encourages humanity to return to.

---

12) Also *Bokbon* (복본): to return to origin, a return to a human nature that was divine and connected.

13) See Appendix 2 on Samshin Philosophy

CHAPTER 8
Leaving Mago's Land

Among those who left Magosung, some were remorseful.
These reappeared outside the walls and asked to return
*   to the land.*
They did not realize their return would only happen according
*   to divine timing.*

Eventually, they began digging around the walls to reach the Earth
*   Milk.*
The land was destroyed, and the Earth Milk spilled all over.
But the people could not drink it—it was immediately absorbed into the
*   hard soil.*

Soon, the Earth Milk began to dry up even for those who remained
*   inside Magosung.*
People grew agitated and fearful of the shortage,
and rushed to consume even more plants and fruits of the land.
This led to even further corruption and chaos, making it difficult to maintain
*   any purity.*

Since Hwang-Gung was the eldest of all humans,
he bound himself in ropes of white grass and appeared before Mago to ask for
forgiveness.
He took responsibility for the Omi Disaster and vowed redemption.

Then, he returned to the people and spoke.

"This disaster of Omi is because those who left Mago do not understand the
Divine Ways and have only increased their fears and doubt. The pureness of
humanity has been destroyed, and now the Magosung itself is in danger. What
are we going to do about this?"

Hearing his words, all four heavenly leaders agreed to form separate clans, living
apart to protect Magosung. Hwang-Gung gave each of them Chunbu [14] *as a*
divine marker, taught them how to harvest arrowroot for food,
and then ordered them to migrate in four directions.

The Chung-Gung clan left from the east gate and went to Unhaeju.
The Baek-So clan left from the west gate and went to Wolshikju.
The Heuk-So clan left from the south gate and went to Sungsengju.
The Hwang-Gung clan left from the north gate and went to Chunsanju.

Chunsanju was a frigid and harsh land.
Hwang-Gung chose this difficult land for its suffering
to pledge his commitment to a return to true nature.

---

14) *Chunbu* (천부) refers to the Divine Ways or the sacred items representing divinity. There is no clear record of what these items were, but they are thought to be a sacred mirror representing the light of the sky, a rattle reproducing heavenly sounds, and a sword for sacred ceremony rituals.

INTERPRETATION

Life for the people who left paradise of Mago's land was difficult. Living outside the walls, they were scared and hungry, and they longed to return. But *Bokbon*—returning to the origin—was only possible if their inner beings reached their divine nature. The people didn't realize this and gathered outside *Magosung*, attempting to force their return. Their actions ended up causing more fear and doubt among the people and created even more chaos and corruption.

Now the entire land of *Magosung* had lost its true divine nature, and people could not continue to live in purity. Hwang-Gung bound himself with white grass (maybe mugwort) at Mago's altar in a ritual vowing to correct this. Using plants and herbs when appearing or communicating with gods has evolved into the use of flowers and herbs in spiritual practices such as ancestral rituals, weddings, and funerals. Korean shamans continue using flowers and herbs in this manner today.

When the four heavenly clans decided to leave *Magosung*, they committed to taking responsibility for the fall of humankind's divine nature and repented their part in the outcome. They also committed to returning to their origin by regaining their true natures of *Sun, Chung,* and *Hu*—goodness, clearness, and generosity. Each clan received a talisman of *Chunbu*, the Divine Ways, to promise this commitment.

There are many opinions on what these talismans were. They likely included a rattle that imitated the heavenly sound of *YulYeo*, a mirror that reflected astral light and awareness, and a sword for use in rituals and ceremonies dedicated to Mago Samshin. These three items have been used for thousands of years by Korean shamans.

When human civilization split into divided clans, the Chung-Gung clan went east to *Unhaeju,* toward the clouds and the ocean. This indicates they traveled east of the Pamir Mountains, or what is present-day southern China and India.

The Baek-So clan went west to *Wolshikju*, where the moon breathes and sets. This indicates they traveled west of the Pamir Mountains to what is present-day Europe.

The Heuk-So clan went south to *Sungsengju*, where stars rise. This indicates they traveled south of the Pamir Mountains to what is present-day Africa and the Middle East.

The Hwang-Gung clan went north to *Chunsanju*, where the sky and mountain meet, where the landscape is said to be quite cold and harsh. This indicates they traveled northeast of the Pamir Mountains to what is present-day northeastern China and Siberia, near Baikal Lake—known by many as the birthplace of Shamanism. Koreans are the descendants of this clan.

When Hwan-Gung and his Gung tribe left, some Baek-So people also followed this tribe, forming their own tribe from the people of the Gung and So tribes. This mixed-blood tribe was later referred to as *Dong Yi Jok* (동이족, Eastern Yi Tribe) in many Chinese historical texts, noted as the ancestral tribe of modern-day Korean people.

CHAPTER 9

The Cleansing of the
Earth, Through the Flood

A thousand years had passed since the people left
 Magosung and settled in different areas.
The descendants of Jiso of the Baek-So clan had left Mago's
 land first and become quite strong.

Most of them had lost their Divine Ways, so they chased and
 attacked those who migrated later than them.
All the clans were separated by the ocean and the mountains, so there
 were few visits among them.

In the meantime, Mago and her daughters repaired the walls of Magosung and
 cleansed the land with celestial water.
Then they relocated above Huhdalsung.

The water used for cleansing overflowed to the east and the west causing a great
 flood that destroyed the land of Unhaeju and killed many people in Wolshikju.

The flood shifted the center of the Earth, creating eclipses and leap years for the
 first time.

INTERPRETATION

Those who left Mago's land lived in tribal cultures for over a thousand years, and some of these tribes thrived. However, they'd lost Mago Samshin's Divine Ways of goodness, clearness, and generosity, so they fought one another violently. Due to the physical distance between them, each tribe lost connection with the others, eventually developing their own languages and cultures in which it was difficult to find commonality.

Water is used not only in Shamanism but in many different religions to purify the body, spirit, and other harmful energies; for example, the baptism of Christians with holy water, the Buddhist *Gwanbul* bathing ritual, and the Wudu purification in Islam. In *Budoji*, the goddesses cleansing their land with celestial water symbolizes the start of using water to purify the impure or unsacred. Another example from Korean Shamanism is the ritual of *Gut*, which contains many forms of using water to cleanse, as shown in *"Chunsu Chigi"* (천수치기, Throwing Divine Water) and Jindo *Ssitkim Gut* (씻김굿, Cleansing Ritual).

In other examples, Mongolian shamans used milk (perhaps because water was rare), and Vietnamese shamans practiced a cleansing ritual, as did tribes near the Himalayas.

The flood has other significance too. The water that went to the east is considered the Pacific Ocean, so perhaps this flood caused the disappearance of the blue-skinned Chung-Gung clan—maybe these are the mythical lands of Lemuria and Atlantis. The water that went to the west is recorded in many ancient traditions describing a great flood—the oldest of which is the Sumerian flood (or the Sumerian creation myth) of Ziusudra. There is also the story of Noah and the Great Flood in the Old Testament.

When the goddesses moved the location of *Magosung* above *Huhdalsung,* this may signify that the Earth had lost its Divine Ways and then existed as a human world. It may also mean the center of Earth (*Magosung*) moved its position to the Big Dipper near the moon.

CHAPTER 10

Hwang-Gung's Promise

Hwang-Gung arrived at Chunsanju
and promised to return to the original nature of Mago.
He had his people continue working on maintaining their
  Divine Ways.

He let his oldest son Yoo-In enlighten the businesses of the human
  world
and let his second and third sons visit all the other tribes.

Then he went into the mountains and became a rock,
where he cried in long, echoing sounds, promising to find ways to return to Mago.

Yoo-In inherited three Chunbu to rule,
and these talismans were such that they could return humanity to
its divine, true nature and become one.

Yoo-In lamented that people were suffering from cold and darkness,
so he taught them how to make fire with the friction of wood and rocks.
People learned to create light, warm their bodies, and cook food.
This made many people very happy.

After Yoo-In ruled for a thousand years, he gave the Chunbu to his son Hwan-In.
Then he went to the mountain to perform rituals and rites to the Sky.
Hwan-In took the three Chunbu and did the work of benefiting humans all over.

The sun was warm and bright; the weather and seasons were in harmony,
many living things were comfortable, and people's beast-like appearances
returned to their former human shapes.

This was thanks to the three generations of Hwang-Gung, Yoo-In, and Hwan-In,
who toiled for three thousand years, depleting almost all of their energy.

INTERPRETATION

Hwang-Gung worked with his clan to understand and teach the Divine Ways (*Chunbu*) and return humanity to its true nature as it was in Mago's land. His oldest son, Yoo-In (유인), was responsible for leading this effort, and his two younger sons traveled far to the other tribes to check on them and help with any challenges.

Hwang-Gung's retirement to the mountains to become a rock refers to Korea's indigenous spiritual practice of praying before large boulders in the mountains. Many Korean shamans and non-Shamanic women have maintained this tradition, memorializing these stones as sacred. Hwang-Gung becoming a rock to enact his promise to help humans return to their original true nature is similar to the Buddhist myth of Kuan Yin choosing not to become a Buddha, instead remaining a Bodhisattva to better help humanity.

Yoo-In took responsibility for the three *Chunbu* talismans. The significance of Yoo-In teaching humanity to use fire is reflected in his name, which means "the one who knows the origin." He is also sometimes referred to as Soo-In, in which *Soo* means flintstone or torch.

After another thousand years of rule, Yoo-In gave the *Chunbu* to his son Hwan-In (환인, also Han-In, 한인) to succeed him. Then, Yoo-In retired to the mountains to teach and perform rituals and rites, which were meant to cleanse bad energies and purify the faults and errors from the lives of human beings. This is considered the beginning of the Korean Shamanic ritual practice of *Gut* (굿) still observed today.

The Samshin philosophy believed to have originated from the *Chunbu* is explained further in Appendix 2.

CHAPTER 11
The Beginning of Hwan-Ung's Baedal Kingdom

Hwan-In's son Hwan-Ung was born with a grand
*   intention.*
He inherited the three Chunbu and performed
*   Purification Rituals.*
He established the Divine Ways so people could understand their
*   origin.*

Because people only focused on their daily livelihoods,
Hwan-Ung created four laws and built an office, Hwan-bu, to enforce them.

The first law was:
People's behavior must be pure and clear.
Avoid becoming evil or harmful unknowingly.
Let people be open and clear to have no obstacles.

The second law was:
Whatever people have accumulated in life will be revisited after death,
so people should not speak impurely or waste carelessly.
People should unite in harmony so there is no conflict or regret.

The third law was:
People who are intolerant, lying, and evil
should be exiled to the desert, so they can purify themselves,
and their evil nature is not left behind in the world.

The fourth law was:
One who commits grave violence and sin should be exiled to Sumra,
and his body burned after death so the remnants of the evil crime
do not remain in the world.

Hwan-Ung also taught people how to build houses, boats, and carriages
so people could live together and travel easily.

The first time Hwan-Ung made a boat and traveled by sea,
he shared the Divine Ways with other tribes,
fostered communication among them,
urged them to not lose their commitment to the Divine Ways,
and taught them to build houses, boats, and carriages and to use fire for cooking.

When Hwan-Ung returned from his travels,
he organized eight sounds and two words and established
Yeok,[15] math, medicine, astrology, and geography.
This benefitted all humans far and wide.

These disciplines taught the Divine Ways within people's everyday lives,
because the distance between people and their disregard for the law had caused
humans to secretly seek to hurt one another for their own benefit.

This initiated a culture of study, teaching, and learning,
because people no longer possessed wisdom innately without first having
to learn it.

---

15) The numerical logic system of all living elements and their changes, including the calendar and timekeeping.

INTERPRETATION

Hwan-Ung (환웅) inherited the Three Divine Talismans of *Chunbu* and performed rituals promising to cleanse the human body and mind from the corruption of the *Omi* Disaster to return humanity to its true nature. He also created laws to help people understand how to do that.

These laws later became the origin of Dangun's founding principle of Ancient Joseon, "*Hongik Ingan* (홍익인간)." Many think the principle of *Hongik Ingan* means "to benefit humans all over the universe." This interpretation may feel impossible to follow to a regular layperson who doesn't possess much power and influence. However, the word *gan* means "between or among," which should be interpreted as "to benefit people among people" to positively influence relationships with others. This interpretation empowers laypeople to follow this wisdom in their day-to-day life.

In the ancient text of *Handangogi,* there were eight laws of Ancient Joseon of Dangun[16], influenced by the laws by Hwan-Ung. These are as follows:

1. The punishment for killing another is the death penalty.

2. Hurting others is punished by a fine of harvest grains.

3. Stealing is punished by giving back the goods and becoming a servant of the family from which one stole, regardless of one's original class.

4. One who damages the sacred altar of the city will be jailed.

5. One who behaves disrespectfully or impolitely will be sent to the military for discipline.

6. One who is lazy and not hardworking will be sent to perform labor.

7. One who commits an obscene crime shall be punished by beating.

---

16) In *Budoji*, Dangun is referred by his name Imgum. Dangun refers to the position of ruler and priest, the name used for the leader of GoJoseon or Ancient Joseon. Imgum is the name of the first Dangun who established Budo, the Divine City.

8. One who cons others shall be released after their admonition. If they repent and admit their wrongdoing voluntarily, their sins will be kept private and not become common knowledge.

Hwan-Ung also organized eight languages and two alphabets. The eight languages were probably the local dialects of the original language spoken in Mago's land. The two alphabets were perhaps the *Garimto* (가림토) letters which later became the basis for Hangul and *Oracle Bone Script* (갑골문자), which later became the basis for Chinese letters.

The *Garimto* alphabet.

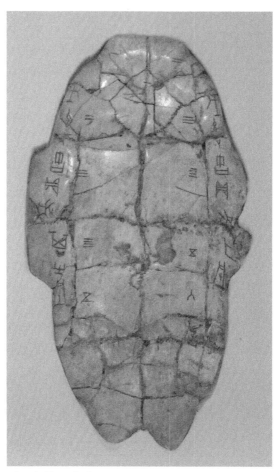

Oracle Bone Script

CHAPTER 12

Imgum Succeeds Hwan-Ung

When Hwan-Ung birthed Imgum,
Tribes all over the world had not yet learned the
    Divine Ways.
People fell into delusion, and the world was full of suffering.

Imgum bore deep concerns for the world,
strived to learn the Divine Ways, performed sacred rituals and cere-
    monies, and thus inherited the Three Talismans of Chunbu.

Imgum taught the people how to farm, breed silkworms, eat arrowroot, and
    fire ceramics.
He promulgated systems for trade, marriage, and keeping genealogical records.
As Imgum ate roots and drank dew, the hairs on his body grew long,
and he traveled all over the world, visiting each tribe one after another.

He traveled for a hundred years, and there was not a place he did not reach.

With the light of the Divine Ways, he cleansed and freed the people from their
    delusions, swearing to return to the true nature of Mago and promising to build
    a Divine City.

*With the migration of people to distant regions, communication was cut off,
and the common language and customs gradually grew different from one
another.*

*Imgum wanted to create a place where all could come together in harmony
and clearly master the Divine Ways.*

*This became the start of people gathering once a month to learn,
because day-to-day life pulled people further from the Divine Ways
and they needed to be taught and reminded so they would not forget again.*

INTERPRETATION

Hwan-Ung birthing Imgum (임검) indicates the transition from Hwan-
Ung's Baedal (배달) kingdom to Imgum's GoJoseon (고조선) kingdom.
Imgum refers not to a role or position but the name of *Dangun Wanggum*
(단군왕검), the founder of Ancient Joseon or GoJoseon, mentioned in the
introduction and the Appendix. Therefore, Imgum, who built the altar to
perform rituals to heaven, eventually became *Dangun Wanggum*, wherein
Dangun refers to the position, meaning a ruler (*gun*) who built the ritual
altar (*dan*) for heaven, and *wang* refers to the word *king*.

Imgum's GoJoseon kingdom followed the following principles:

- *Hongik Ingan* (홍익인간): To broadly benefit and nurture humans
  among humans (relationships between humans).

- *Jese Ihwa* (제세이화): To find enlightenment through the Divine
  Ways and spread it across the land.

- *Seongtong Gwangmyeong* (성통광명): To return to the original true
  human nature, so all can find enlightenment.

Imgum also improved living standards by teaching about farming,
weaving, foraging, fishing, pottery, and trading. He also initiated the
practice of recording births and keeping family trees so people could

remember their ancestors. When one's parents died, people were taught to grieve with specific ritualistic acts performed three days past death, three months past, one year past, and three years after death. These rituals eventually influenced the funeral and ancestral traditions of Confucianism.

Imgum primarily ate foraged herbs and roots and drank spring water, so his soul was clear and thoughts peaceful, drawing him closer to the energy of deities. He is said to have worn a blue robe, with his hair in a long braid. He visited tribal villages for a hundred years, offering teachings and reminding tribes of the Divine Ways, repeating the lesson of the *Omi* Disaster, and encouraging people to recover their true nature of goodness, clearness, and generosity. He also promised to build a sacred city where all could gather and perform rituals to honor and connect with Mago Samshin.

CHAPTER 13

Imgum Builds Budo,
the Divine City

Imgum returned and chose the land upon which to build
  the sacred city of Budo.
It was to the northeast where the magnet pointed.
This was a central location where two and six communed, and
  four and eight combined to bear fruit.

Bright mountains and clear waters stretched for a thousand miles.
Ocean and land connected and spread into ten directions, where nine
  and one—the end and beginning, could continue cycling.

Ginseng, pine nuts, and seven-color jade stones were plentiful all around, rooted
  in the heart of the main river.
This was a fertile, blessed land where the energies of one, three, five, and seven
  gathered to manifest material things.

Imgum built the sacred altar Chunbudan on the bright mountaintop of
  Mt. Taebaeksan,
and supportive Bodan altars in all four directions.
Each Bodan was connected by waterways a thousand miles long,
and the waterways were protected by two gates at each end.

This was modeled after Magosung.

Below the altars, villages were built, lakes were formed near the coasts, and four docks and four ports surrounded the city a thousand miles from east to west. Six Bu staging stations were built between the docks and the ports, where many tribes could gather and live together.

Finally, Budo was complete. It was magnificent, beautiful, and bright with light. It was enough to become the heartland of the people.

INTERPRETATION

This Divine City built by Imgum was Budo, and the city's central area was where rituals to Heaven were performed. Budo, the Divine City with the sacred altar *Chunbudan* (천부단), was specially chosen as the one and only place where humans could perform rituals and connect with the sky. It was the most sacred and central place in all aspects (economic and spiritual) for all the surrounding tribes.

Inspired by the former construction of *Magosung*, the central altar was *Chunbudan*. In four directions stood *Bodan* (보단, supportive altars) that protected the main altar and functioned as the main altar when needed. Between these *Bodan* altars were waterways to prevent attacks and provide transportation for faraway clans to reach Budo easily. Around these *Bodans,* villages formed for people to gather and live.

The wisdom of ancient numerology, astronomy, and geography was used to select the Divine City's ground. The altar was built in a directional relationship to the Big Dipper, where it rises or falls. The magnet pointed to the northeast, thought to be where the Big Dipper rose.

In ancient *Yeok* (역), two represents south and fire, and six represents north and water. Four represents west and metal, and eight represents east and tree. One signified the beginning, nine indicated the end, and water constantly flowed from one to nine, meaning this was a land that supported the continued cycles of life. This chosen land was where all these numbers, directions, and natural elements were balanced in harmony.

Another purpose of building Budo was so people living far apart could stay in contact, be reminded of their shared origins, and feel connected. In Budo, people could be reminded of and learn about the Divine Ways and stay connected. With the distance and development of their own cultures and languages, it was difficult for them to remember their common roots and shared goal of returning to the true state of Mago's paradise.

Modern Koreans continue to perform the ancestral rituals that began in Budo on the days of their parents' deaths. The purpose of the ancestral traditions is not only to honor the ancestors but also to facilitate grown children gathering once a year to connect, find harmony, and stay close.

Once completed, Budo became the heartbeat of the people. It's the place where people could learn *Chunbu* and practice the teachings of Mago Samshin. Finally, during Imgum's leadership, this city was created to perform rituals to the sky and to educate people.

CHAPTER 14
The Rise of Budo

Thus Hwang-Gung's descendants of sixty thousand
  migrated to Budo.
They felled trees to make eighty thousand rafts carved with
  the sacred sigil,
and set off on the water of Chunji, inviting the tribes from all
  around.

Tribes saw the rafts carved with the sacred sigil and gathered one by one,
and held a big Shinshi [17] in the birch forest.
There, they cleared their minds with a cleansing ritual, observed the movement
  of the sky, studied Mago's bloodline to know the descending tribes,
and organized a spoken and written language according to the melody of Chunbu.

They also determined the position of the North Star and the Big Dipper,
burned sacrificial offerings on top of the stone altar in ritual performance,
and gathered to sing and play the music of Chun-Ung. [18]

---

17) The sacred festival gathering, comprised of the ritual to the sky, a market for trading, and opportunities to share information, language, and customs.

18) Hwan-Ung.

All the tribes dug precious jade from the Banggon Cave at Mt. Bangjangsan,
carved the Chunbu sigil and called it Bangjang haein,
and controlled and cleared the seven conflicts before returning home.

After that, every ten years, Shinshi opened without fail.
Through this, the languages became similar, and laws became one.
People largely harmonized.

Accordingly, they built shrines near the beach to revere and serve the Divine Ways,
They let the tribes visit or settle on the land around them.
From this, for a thousand years, Sunghwang spread far and wide.

INTERPRETATION

After establishing Budo, Imgum relocated sixty thousand descendants of Hwang-Gung living near *Chunsanju* (modern-day Siberia around Lake Baikal) and sent out eight thousand rafts carved with the sacred symbol of Mago Samshin to invite all descending tribes to Budo. Pictured here is the sigil: three small circles within a larger circle,

Budo's Samshin Pattern.

representing Mago Samshin—with the large circle signifying the universe and three small circles representing the Triple Goddess Samshin. It's a sigil that looks like the sacred symbols of other ancient faiths, like those of the Druids, Buddhists, Christians, and Hindus. One can imagine that the design of the sacred symbol of Mago Samshin was intended to represent the belief that humanity started from *Magosung.*

Ancient Celtic Triskele.

Symbol of Sambo of Korean Buddhism.

Held in Budo every ten years, *Shinshi* (신시) was a sacred festival gathering that included a ritual to the sky, a market for trading, and sharing of information, language, and cultures—not unlike festivals held today. It allowed many different clans to gather and learn from one another. Naturally, the market was formed to facilitate the exchange of native goods, services, entertainment, and art. Even after the disappearance of Budo, some ancient records show the Silla Dynasty (57–935 CE) continued to hold *Shinshi* in various regions of southern Korea.

Madonna Oriflamma, Banner of Peace by Nochiolas Roerich.

Historically, the work of shamans was initiated and performed by sacred leaders: specifically, Hwan-In, Hwan-Ung, and Dangun. Those who performed rituals during *Shinshi* were called *mudangs*, the Korean shamans. Today, the concept of *Shinshi* continues to be threaded through festivals, entertainment, and sports games. However, these modern gatherings are missing the critical element of ritual, intended to cleanse and bless the events.

Sunghwang (성황) were sacred altars and shrines found in less-populated, perhaps more remote regions of Korea, where villages could perform their own rituals every year instead of waiting for *Shinshi* to be hosted at Budo once a decade.

CHAPTER 15

Budo's Economy and Rituals

At the intersection of the Ye and Yang rivers, Joshi
was founded,
and Haeshi at the eight lakes near the coasts.
Here, the Joje Ritual was performed every October,
where all tribes made offerings of their local goods.

Tribes from the mountains made offerings of deer and sheep,
and tribes from the seas made offerings of fish and shellfish.
They prayed, "We offer the sacrifice of fish and sheep at the altar.
Please cleanse the blood of Omi so the calamity of the living may end!"
This was indeed the Joseon Je Ritual.

At the time, people living near the mountains ate a lot of fish and meat, so the
products traded most often were dried meat, shellfish, and animal skins.
Therefore by performing a sacrificial ritual, people could atone and express gratitude.

They dipped their fingers in blood to recognize the value of life,
And poured the blood onto earth to repay the grace of being reared.
This was to atone for the sins of Omi and prevent further disasters through sacrifi-
cial offering, which confessed the sufferings of the human body and mind.

At the annual ritual, there was a great increase in goods.
Large markets, called Haeshi, were held near docks and ports.
There, they purified bad energy, cleansed their bodies, observed their natural
*   surroundings, and established trade rules, like setting the prices, measurements,*
*   and uses of goods.*

They dug channels similar to Budo's eight major waterways,
performed rituals and divination near the waters,
and gathered together to celebrate and pray for abundance and prosperity.

All the tribes obtained pine nuts from the peak of Mt. Bongraesan Wonkyo,
called them Bongrae Haesong and gratefully returned home with them.
From then on, there continued lively trading and production of goods, and there
*   was abundance all around.*

INTERPRETATION

Joshi were small, inland *Shinshi* that were easier to get to, where people performed rituals and exchanged local goods from the inland.

Haeshi were small *Shinshi* at the waterways and coasts, where fish were exchanged and offered in ritual.

Joje was the shortened name of *Joseon Je*, the largest ritual performed at *Shinshi*, honoring the sun, moon, stars, sky, and Mago.

Since most of the local goods from mountain and ocean clans were fish and meat, which necessitated the killing of life, the tribes performed a sacrificial ritual with the animal's blood to cleanse them of their sins.

The largest ritual and market was hosted every Lunar New Year. People cleansed their bodies before rituals and then worked on pricing and trading goods. There was also a thanksgiving ritual to celebrate the harvest and distribute the harvest bounty among the people—what later became *Chuseok*, the fall harvest festival still celebrated in modern Korea today.

CHAPTER 16
Budo's Specialty

People who came to Budo obtained
a three-rooted sacred plant from the Mt. Daeyo[19] *valley*
  in Yeongju,[20] *and this was ginseng.*
They called it Yeongju Haesam, which signified the preserva-
  tion of Three Virtues, and returned home with it.

Ginseng has distinct lifecycles and shapes
and those from Jasak province live especially long.
Dormant for a season of forty years,
then gathering energy for thirteen more forty-year seasons,
after four additional cycles, it bears seeds and flowers.
Such a plant was not available anywhere other than Budo.

It was called Bangsakcho, what's known as the medicine of immortality.
Even the smallest root had sacred power if it originated from Budo,

---

19) Ancient records describe Mt. Daeyo as one of five sacred mountains where deities lived, in the middle of oceans to the east of the Balhae kingdom (698-926 CE).

20) Another name referring to Samshin. Also a mystical land in the middle of the ocean. Jeju Island's ancient name was also *Yeongju*.

so people who visited the city made sure to obtain some.

Therefore, the area's specialties were the three-rooted sacred ginseng, the five-leafed auspicious pine nuts, and the seven-color precious jade stones.

These were the blessings from heaven for the people of the Budo.

INTERPRETATION

Sacred ginseng was thought to have the power to bring the medicine of the Three Virtues of Samshin — goodness, clearness, and generosity. (See Chapter 10). Obtaining the Three Virtues was done by improving people's minds, souls, and bodies; this ginseng was powerful medicine to help with that. Only ginseng produced on the path of the Big Dipper was thought to have the sacred medicinal power of Samshin, and much of the Korean peninsula falls on this path.

Budo's ginseng matured over one period of forty years, during which it lay dormant. Then it gathered energy for thirteen more forty-year seasons (520 years) before flowering after four final cycles of 520 years (a total of 2080 years.) Budo's ginseng was indeed a rare and powerful medicinal plant.

CHAPTER 17
The Rise of Yao

At this time, Yao[21] arose south of the sacred mountain.
He was a descendant of the people who made the first
*   exodus from Mago's land.*

He had visited the gatherings for Budo rituals,
and learned the Divine Ways from the leaders of the western
*   territories.*

However, he was not diligent in numeric wisdom
and did not understand the logic of a sequence of nine numbers with five in
*   the center.*
Mistakenly, he thought that the five in the middle and the other eight numbers on
*   the outside meant that one number ruled all others—*
designed to control all outside from one inside.

Therefore, he created the Law of Five Elements and established a kingdom
*   for himself.*

---

21) In the ancient Chinese myth, it said Yao founded the *Law of Five Elements* from the patterns on the shell of a sacred turtle. He is believed to be the founder of the ancient Chinese
culture and the kingdoms. *Budoji* tells a different version of his origin.

But the wisemen Sobu[22] and Heoyu opposed this vehemently and refused.

Yao finally left, gathering people to attack Budo and drive out the descendants of Myo.
The Myo tribe were descendants of Hwang-Gung, and their land was the homeland of Yoo-in.

Because Imgum had left Budo and sent groups of people to visit other tribes, Yao took the opportunity to attack Myos' land, and people were displaced to the east, west, and north.

Yao then divided the land into nine states and called it a kingdom,
positioned himself in the center as the emperor,
and established his own capital city to confront Budo.

Using the words said to come from a turtle and
the existence of sacred flowers as a divine prophecy,
he created a new Yeok[23] for himself
abolishing the ways of Chunbu and rejecting Budo's Yeok.
This was the second calamity of the human world.

---

22) It is said that Sobu refused Yao's proposal to become the next emperor by saying his ears were dirtied from the proposal, washing his ears in the river. When Heoyu heard what happened, he said, "How can I feed this dirtied water to my cattle?" and moved upstream to feed his cattle there.

23) Yeok is the numerical logic system, or law, of all living elements and their changes, including the calendar and clock. This new system included the Five Elements of fire, water, tree, earth, and metal. This was different from what Budo believed, which developed its system from the four original clans of Mago, who oversaw four elements: fire, water, earth, and air.

CHAPTER 18

Yoo-ho is Sent to Address Yao

This second calamity worried Imgum greatly, and he
*   ordered Yoo-in's [24] descendant Yoo-ho and his sons,*
*   along with approximately one hundred officials and*
*   soldiers, to visit Yao to persuade him.*

Yao received them politely and obeyed their words,
and had them stay near the waters of Habin.

Yoo-ho quietly observed the situation, taught the people,
and moved his residence several times.

Before, when Yoo-ho lived in Budo, he only ate arrowroots and did not eat
*   five flavors.*
Therefore he was ten feet tall with eyes shining like fire.
He was older than Imgum by a hundred years, and he followed the work of his
*   ancestors in assisting Imgum in teaching the Divine Ways.*

---

24) Hwang-Gung's oldest son, who succeeded him after their migration out of Mago's paradise.
See Chapter 10.

He had now become a diplomat, attempting to save a world that had become stubborn and unreasonable. But he faced many difficulties.

At this time, Yao observed the character of Yoo-ho's son Yoo-shun and had a different intention in mind.
He pretended to collaborate with him, trusting him with work, all while attempting to seduce him with his two daughters.
Yoo-shun was finally persuaded.[25]

Earlier, Yoo-shun had become an official of Hwanbu to enforce Budo's laws, yet he had not appropriately performed for reasons varying from excess to lack. Now he fell to the temptation of Yao, marrying Yao's two daughters in secret and covertly taking sides with Yao, helping him.

---

25) Yao persuaded Yoo-shun to support him by offering more power, and offered his own two daughters Ahwang and Yuhyoung, in marriage with Yoo-shun. In contrast, ancient Chinese myths tell many different versions of the story of Emperor Shun, or *the Great Shun*, and his life, work, and relationship with Yao and Yao's two daughters who became empresses.

CHAPTER 19

The Fall of Yao and Shun and The Rise of Xia

While Yoo-ho tried to have words with Yoo-shun, he
   only said "yes, yes" and did not change.
Shun finally came to serve Yao by searching for wisemen to
   kill them,
then attacking and wiping out the remaining members of the
   Myo tribe.

Yoo-ho could not ignore this any longer.
He criticized and attacked Shun.
Shun called out to the sky, lamenting.
Yao did not have anywhere to go, so he gave his throne to Shun and dis-
   missed himself.

Yoo-ho said,
"Omi's disaster is not yet finished, and he made a calamity of the Oheng.[26]
The land is full of sin, the north star has faded in the sky, and many things are
   damaged. Humans are suffering. How can I ignore correcting it?
After all, one may forgive and teach a person who sins without knowing.

---

26) The Five Elements.

*However, one cannot forgive a person who knowingly sins, even if he is a close
family member."*

*He ordered his second son, Yoo-sang, to assemble soldiers, announce his brother's
sins, and attack.*

After many years of war, they destroyed the city.

*Yao died while imprisoned, and Shun escaped to the fields of Chango with his
soldiers dispersing in all directions to escape.*

*Yu was a leader following Yao and had wanted to avenge his father's death
by Yoo-shun,*

so he chased Shun and killed him.

Shun's two wives then killed themselves by throwing themselves into the river.

*Yu said, "Justice has been established through my efforts,"
appeasing the people and soldiers before returning home.*

Yoo-ho observed Yu's actions quietly from a distance.

Then Yu moved to a new city, assembling soldiers and gathering more weapons.

He eventually disobeyed Yoo-ho, ultimately calling himself the emperor of Xia.

INTERPRETATION

Married to the two daughters of Yao, Yoo-shun followed his father-in-law's
requests and began to covet power and wealth instead of acting within his
role as Budo's official. He killed many local wisemen because they were
vocal in their opposition to his decisions. He drove away members of the
Myo tribe and killed others since they were living in abundance, as the
first tribe to master rice farming. Taking over their territory and resources
gave Yoo-shun even greater power and stability.

Finally, Yoo-ho could not stand any more destruction and went
after Yoo-shun in what was perhaps the original war between father and
son—a war between a father committed to teaching and preserving the
Divine Ways of Budo and a son who only wanted to use the new way of

Five Elements to give himself power and control. This war took longer than expected.

The biggest reason Yoo-ho attacked Yao was that his Five Element principle created a kingdom wherein one center ruled all others. The longer the people followed this new system, the more they would forget Mago's foundation and principles.

Once war broke out, Yao claimed to have retired by hiding away and abdicating his kingship to Yoo-shun. Shun was distraught about the war against his own family and lamented toward the sky, crying out his sorrows. However, Yao continued to control Shun behind the scenes.

Once Yoo-ho ordered his second son, Yoo-sang, to attack Yao and Yoo-shun, their city was finally destroyed over many years. Yao died while in exile, and Shun was killed by his own soldiers, led by Yu, though he attempted to flee from the attack.

After killing then-king Yoo-shun, Yu acted like he was a hero who'd faked loyalty to Shun in order to finally assassinate him, all for the good of Budo. But Yoo-ho did not trust him, instead quietly observing his actions. Yu then relocated to a region where he could create his own empire, named it Xia, and rose against Yoo-ho.

CHAPTER 20

Yoo-ho Tries to Persuade Yu

Yu finally deserted Budo and built an altar in the
mountains, conquering many tribes in the west and
the south.
He then called them lords, and gathered them at the prominent
mountain to receive their offerings.
This was copying Budo's ways, but it was done suddenly and
violently.

With the world becoming loud and chaotic, many people took refuge in
Budo.
So, Yu cut off land and water routes leading to Budo to prevent migration.
However, he did not dare attack Budo.

During this time, Yoo-ho remained in the western territory away from Budo.
The Myo tribe reassembled, connected with descendants of Sobu and Heoyu
and with many other tribes in the south and the west.
Its power became so great that it established its own state.

Yoo-ho finally sent an official to Yu to persuade him:

"Yao misunderstood the divine numerology.
He divided the land according to his whim, using the opportunity for personal
  gains, building himself an altar and raising livestock, and driving away the
  native people.
He called himself an emperor to rule as he wished.
The people have fallen as silent as dirt, rock, and plants,
and the Divine Ways have grown impotent.
This is merely the fulfillment of personal greed using lies and the stolen authority
  of Heaven.

"If it is true that the emperor may replace the divineness of the heaven, then
  shouldn't he surely be able to move the sun and moon and create all things in
  the world? The emperor reflects the truth of divine numerology. It is not something a person can claim with lies. If falsely claimed, then it becomes an ugly
  game of empty deceit.

"The purpose of humanity is to realize and understand the Divine Truth, and the
  purpose of this world is to bring light to the truth and wisdom.
What else is there than this? Budo's law is to clearly understand the Divine Ways
  so people may live their original purpose and receive the virtues of its blessings.

"Therefore among people who speak and listen, there may be a before and after,
but there is no high and low.
Among people who give and receive, there may be closeness and distance,
but there is no forcing in or pushing out.
Therefore, there is equality among people all around
and all tribes behave in accordance with their own.

"Only the salvation of Omi's Disaster and a return to the Chunbu of the great
  Magosung is an endeavor worthy of being overseen by one person who sacrifices
  themself to the task.
Not every person can handle this task, so since the old times, this endeavor did not
  coincide with other businesses of the human world. The examples of Hwang-
  Gung and Yoo-In demonstrate this."

INTERPRETATION

Yu defied Budo by creating his own ritual altar and giving himself the right of power to communicate with heaven. After conquering the nearby tribes, he assembled them to make offerings at the ritual. This was a very different way of operating from that of Budo.

Budo, created by Imgum, was established to teach the Divine Ways to help return humanity to its true nature. In contrast, the purpose of Yu's city was to increase his power and wealth at the expense of other people.

In Budo, leftover ritual offerings were traded among the tribes, naturally creating a market that helped everyone's economy and livelihood. But Yu only used the ritual performance as a method to accumulate his wealth.

Yu's violent attempt to attack neighboring tribes and use their members as slaves to increase his economic gain created a system of slavery. Many tribespeople left the area to seek refuge in Budo. Yu, in return, closed all communication and travel between the cities. Yu's Xia kingdom grew independently, but he didn't dare attack Budo.

Yoo-ho finally sent a diplomat to Yu and tried to convince him of the importance of maintaining the integrity of the Divine Ways of leading and teaching the people.

CHAPTER 21

The Faults of the Five Element Philosophy Explained

Yoo-ho laid out his case against the Five Element
   Philosophy, saying,
"As far as the so-called Oheng,[27] *there is no such law in the*
   principles of divine numerology. The situation of five as the
   center represents an intersection of all directions, not some-
   thing that changes and moves.

"All numbers from one to nine change and move, so five is not always at
   the center.
When all nine numbers cycle and combine with YulYeo,
all things are created.

"When five and seven move in a cycle,
that cycle is not limited to five; four and seven also appear in the cycle.
In Yoonmyeok,[28] *four is found in the center, not five.*
This is because all nine numbers don't change their nature.
When Yoonmyeok finishes one cycle, it is 28 of seven, not five.

---

27) The Five Elements.

28) A formula of multiplying one number by itself, eg. $3 \times 3 \times 3 \times 3$.

"Also, in the pairing of the elements of all things: metal, tree, water, fire, earth,
why separate metal and earth?
If you try to separate them by the minuscule differences between the two,
Then why not distinguish air, wind, grass, and stone as their own elements too?

"Once you start dividing elements, the divisions will become never-ending.
Correct counting indicates there are only four elements. But not five elements.
Why pair the characteristics of elements with the characteristics of numbers?
The characteristics of elements are based on nine numbers, not five.

"Therefore, this Oheng is truly absurd.
This is a false modification of the truth of the human world, therefore creating
   conflict with the Divine. How can I not be afraid?"

INTERPRETATION

Oheng, or the Five Elements Philosophy, taught that the numeral five always existed at the center, ruling all other numbers. In the numerology followed in Budo, the center was not always five but was fluid to other numbers like one, seven, and nine because all numbers were considered part of a dynamic cycle. Since all things in the universe are created through the flow and cycle of all nine numbers, the centralized power cannot be static—not only five but also four and seven.

Furthermore, in contrast to the four original elements of water, fire, air, and earth, the Five Elements wrongly split up the earth elements into earth, tree, and metal, which can deceive people and prevent them from learning the Divine Truth of the universe.

CHAPTER 22

A Critique of the *Yeok* System of Yao's Five Elements

"And about Yeok, instead of observing the fundamentals
  of divine numbers,
he took the fundamentals from the back of a turtle or the
  petals of Myunghyup.[29]
What were Yao's intentions?

"All things in the world come from numbers, and each is represented
  by a number,
So why has Yao only chosen to use a turtle and a sacred plant
if all things in the world have their own numerical system?

"Yao's Yeok is, therefore, merely that of a turtle and a plant, not
  of humanity,
it obviously does not correspond to the human world.

"Yet Yao forced humans to fit into his structure,
even overturning the three months of the calendar.

---

29) Sacred flowers thought to grow one petal every moon cycle, said to have been found by
Yao. The discovery of this sacred flowering plant was considered the divine validation of his Five
Element philosophy.

He brought divine confusion into the elemental system,
because Yeok is the all-encompassing system of all lives in the universe.

"When Yeok is correct, there is balance and harmony between the Divine Ways
and human business, so it acts as a blessing.
But when Yeok is wrong, it acts as a curse against Divine Ways.
It is through the correctness or the wrongness of Yeok that the good or bad of the
human world is established.
How can I not fear?

"A long time ago, one person's doubt led to the Omi Disaster
which still affects all people after all these years.
Now the disaster of Yeok threatens to overturn the Divine Truth of the world and
its future—
I fear this greatly."

INTERPRETATION

This chapter describes how the Five Element Philosophy disputed and threatened to destroy the Divine Ways from Mago.

It did so first by using the pattern of the turtle shell and sacred flower petals as the foundational design, misrepresenting divine numerology and corrupting its significance.

Second, *Oheng* (Five Element) philosophy suggested humankind depended on the elements of the physical world, ruled by one figure in the center to whom they were subservient, paid taxes, and more.

Third, by establishing a moon-based calendar, *Oheng* philosophy shifted human rhythms and consciousness from following the sun to following the moon.

CHAPTER 23

Budo's *Yeok* System Explained

"The Divine Ways rotate through cycles, so there is a
  beginning and end within itself.
When the cycle is completed four times, then there is yet
  another beginning and end.

"The cycle of one beginning and end is called small Yeok,
two cycles of beginning and end are called middle Yeok,
and four repetitions of beginning and end are called large Yeok.

"One cycle of small Yeok is one year of 12 months,
in which each month has 28 days separated into four weeks of seven days each.
There are 52 weeks in one year, therefore totaling 364 days.
This results from a combination of the numerals one, four, and seven.

"At the beginning of each year, a large ritual is held, lasting another full day, so
  that makes 365 days in each year.

"Every three and a half years, there is a great movement of the moon,
and this is the law of numbers two, five, and eight.
This movement equals one additional day, so every fourth year lasts 366 days.

"Every ten and a half years are movements called Gu, which are the foundation of time.

300 Gu make 1 Myo, and Myo is the observation of Gu's movements.

So 9,633 Myo make up the seconds, minutes, and hours of one day,

through a combination of three, six, and nine.

"In this way, the cycles of beginning and end reach the middle and large Yeok, in order, resulting in the creation of rational numerology.

"Yao's three wrongdoings[30] *came from vain desires only for himself.*

How can you compare them to the true Divine Ways of Budo?

False truth will eventually fail because it lacks inner rationale,

but Divine Truth will persevere because it holds plenty of rationales inside."

INTERPRETATION

The lunar calendar is comprised of 28-day months and 12-month years. This is in accordance with women's menstruation, or "moon" cycles. Therefore, it is thought that the moon receives masculine energy from the sun and then reflects onto earth as feminine energy.

One week consists of seven days, initially influenced by the seven-day ritual of human wholeness, which included praying to Samshin three times during a seven-day period. Korean shamans continue this tradition of three-by-seven days prayer via 21-day prayers. Koreans avoid visiting newborns for 21 days after birth to avoid sharing bad energies. After 21 (three-by-seven) days, the babies are considered whole humans who can be visited freely. This practice further demonstrates the significance of numerals three, seven, and 21.

---

30) The three wrongdoings of Yao were establishing a centralized emperorship, creating the Five Elements philosophy, and inventing the new *Yeok* that conflicted with the divine system of Budo.

CHAPTER 24
Xia Drives Out Yoo-ho

Though Yoo-ho firmly tried to persuade Yu to end his
rule and return to Budo,
Yu was obstinate and did not listen.

In return, Yu believed Yoo-ho was threatening and insulting him
and instead attacked Yoo-ho multiple times with his soldiers.
But even after many battles, he did not win and finally died near
the encampment near Mt. Mo.

Xia's people, who controlled the flood with Yu in the past, [31] *were angered and*
saddened by Yu's death. Those wanting to fight to the death to avenge his death
numbered in the tens of thousands.

Yu's son Qi led these troops to attack Yoo-ho again. Yoo-ho's troops numbered only
in the thousands, but Xia's troops still could not win after multiple battles.

---

31) According to ancient Chinese records, Yu was the founder of the Xia empire and the final
emperor of the ancient Yao-Shun-Yu era. During the reign of emperor Shun there were nine
years of flooding and Yu was ordered to control the flood. When he did well, Shun gave Yu the
role of his successor. In ancient times, someone who could control flooding and the water element was thought to be the wisest sage and often became king.

Qi finally took down his encampment and did not try to attack again.
The people of Xia were restless and angered.

Yoo-ho saw that the Xia people had been blinded by Yu and would not be corrected quickly.
He left for the southwest with his troops to teach various tribes instead, and Yooho's stronghold disappeared on its own.

CHAPTER 25
Yoo-ho's Futile Efforts to Teach People

With this, the Taewon region south of the sacred moun-
tain became chaotic.
Both the king and his people were blind to the truth, and an
age of darkness ensued,
as the strong positioned themselves at the top of society, and the
weak fell to the bottom.

Then a terrible law was put in place that placed ownership of all lands to
the king and lords,
thus oppressing the people beneath them and spreading like an insidious illness.

People invaded lands and pillaged their neighbors, gathering in gangs to kill
one another.
There was no longer any goodness in the world.
This is how both the Xia and Shang dynasties fell, yet the people didn't
realize why.

All because they severed their ties with Budo and no longer knew the Divine Ways.

*Yoo-ho gathered his people and arrived at the lands of Wolshik and Sungseng,[32]
the homelands of the Baek-So and Heuk-So clans.
The descendants of both clans maintained the tradition of building So,[33] con-
structing many tall towers and stairs.*

*Yet they had forgotten the original sound of Chunbu and did not understand the
Divine Truth of building those towers. The Divine Ways were misunderstood,
and people were jealous of one another, doubted each other, and attacked
one another frequently. Mago's ways were corrupted, disappeared, or became
meaningless.*

*Yoo-ho visited many villages and tried to explain Mago's way and the principles
of Chunbu, but the tribes doubted him and did not accept his teachings.
Regrettably, only those responsible for the old ways[34] came to receive his words.
Yoo-ho only spoke to them, asking them to pass the information on.*

INTERPRETATION

The ancient people of Korea originated from Mago Samshin and
received the divine wisdom of the Three Virtues of goodness, clearness,
and generosity. After humanity left *Magosung*, the people who had preserved the ancient wisdom and understood how to return to the true
nature of *Magosung* traveled far to spread this knowledge—they were
first called *Sam Lang*.

Although these traveling teachers were referred to by different names
at different eras of history, their ultimate goal remained consistent: to

---

32) When leaving *Magosung*, the Baek-So clan went to *Wolshikju*, where the moon breathes and
sets. This indicates they traveled to the west of the Pamir Mountains, what is present-day Europe.
The Heuk-So clan went to *Sungsengju*, where stars rise. This indicates they went to the south of
the Pamir Mountains, what is present-day Africa and the Middle East.

33) A high structure for dwelling or spiritual purpose, like pyramids.

34) Shamans, or rite keepers.

restore humanity to its true divine state and return to Mago's paradise, ultimately freeing humanity from its doubts and fears.

Throughout Korea's ancient history, groups of these teachers were dedicated to learning *Chunbu* and the teachings of Mago Samshin to pass the wisdom on to future generations. These groups were divided over two shared purposes: those who worked to gain and disseminate knowledge and those who practiced ancient rituals and rites amongst the people. During the Baedal kingdom of Hwan-Ung, these teachers were called *Sam Lang*. In the North Buyeo kingdom, they went by the name *Chunwang-rang*. In Goguryeo, they were *Joeui Sun-in*; in Baekjae, *Mujeol*; in Silla, *Hwarang*; in Goryeo, *Sun-rang*; and in Joseon, *Sunbi*.

These were the ancient shamans and *mudangs*. Yet, these teachers also lost their Divine Ways over time and could no longer perform their duties properly. One can only wonder when humanity will return to Mago's paradise.

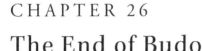

CHAPTER 26
The End of Budo

Imgum had heard of all of Yoo-ho's efforts and appreci-
ated his work.
He resettled Yoo-ho's tribes and put them to work in the
official area of Budo.
But Imgum still worried about the state of the world intensely
and went into the mountains to pray for a return to the
Divine Truth.

Imgum's son Buru succeeded with the three Chunbu talismans and ruled Budo,
announcing that heaven and earth come from oneness and that all humanity
is one tribe.
He honored the wisdom of the ancestors and practiced the Divine Ways of Hwan-
Ung to benefit and improve people's lives in the world.

He kept close to many neighboring tribes and tried to return them to the
Divine Ways,
however, the other way [35] gained strength rapidly, and he was unable to accom-
plish his goal.

---

35) The Five Elements and the unitary Chinese emperorship.

Buru eventually passed the Chunbu on to his son Eupru and went into the
   mountains.

Eupru was born with a compassionate spirit and had great intentions when he accepted
   the Chunbu. He pitied the people of Xia and other tribes falling into chaos and distress,
and was saddened that the Divine Truth had fallen to a land ruled by lies.

Finally, he locked away the Chunbu inside the altar of the bright land
and went into the mountains, focused only on praying for humanity's return to its
   true nature.
He didn't return for a hundred years, and the people he left behind cried in distress.

Imgum was born at the beginning of the time after Mago
and established Budo to preserve the example of the Divine Ways.
For a thousand years, his work was extensive and dedicated.

But then came the time when the succession of Chunbu was interrupted.
Since they first migrated out of Mago's land, seven generations of teachers:
Hwang-Gung, Yoo-in, Hwan-In, Hwan-Ung, Imgum, Buru, and Eupru succeeded
   one another in preserving the Divine Ways of Chunbu—for seven thousand years.

INTERPRETATION

Today, few people study or practice the wisdom of the Samshin, but one can speculate the many organized religions of the modern world were rooted in the wisdom of Samshin ways. The branches of the world's organized religions are rooted in Samshin, yet these branches have lost their roots and forgotten their origins. This is why there are many conflicts and much suffering in the world.

Returning to the Three Virtues of Mago Samshin—goodness, clearness, and generosity—by embracing the ancient Korean roots and traditions survived by Korea's Shamanism may help the people of today's world experience a greater connection to the Divine and heal from generations of suffering.

ILLUSTRATIONS

"Homecoming" illustrates a vision of Budo in the panorama of Korea's sacred blue mountains. A stone stacked altar sits atop the central mountain where a ritual is being performed and the people are being taught the old ways. The painting is based on the artist's visit to Mt. Jirisan and *Chonje-dan*, where rituals honoring the Divine have been continuously performed for centuries.

Image by Meesha Goldberg

"Mago & the Universal Vibration" envisions the creation of the world. Divine vibrations swirl and catalyze life from the celestial bodies as Mago hovers in the cosmic field overlooking her two daughters. According to *Budoji*, the harmony of the world is maintained by these vibrations, and by returning to the original teachings, balance may be restored.

Image by Meesha Goldberg

"Budo's Sacred Medicine" illustrates ginseng, pine, and jade, the three abundant treasures that were "blessings from Heaven for the people of Budo." These gifts of nature are highly valued to this day for their nutrition and potency, and had additional esoteric significance that gave them sacred value. The symbol of three circles contained within one circle is a symbol of Mago and her two daughters as the archetypal Triple Goddess, Samshin.

Image by Meesha Goldberg

APPENDICES

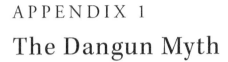

APPENDIX 1

The Dangun Myth

THE DANGUN MYTH AND THE FOUNDING OF GOJOSEON (ANCIENT JOSEON)

Often, specific myths or fables are used to tell the birth
stories of leaders of ancient kingdoms or belief systems.
This is because they were thought to represent Heaven (the
sky) and utilize its power to rule the people, therefore claiming
the divine right of kings.[36] This is also the case in the founding
myth of Korea's people.

The mythology of Hwan-Ung (also called Han-Ung), who started
the kingdom of Baedal, and Dangun, who succeeded him and founded
GoJoseon, is as follows.

---

36) The right and power to rule as given by heaven. Also, kings were often considered to be
divine.

A long time ago, Hwan-In knew that his divine son[37] *Hwan-Ung was interested in the human world under the sky. He looked down around Mt. Taebaeksan and saw an appropriate place to build a kingdom from which he could reign. So he sent Hwan-Ung down with three Chunbu-in.*[38]

Hwan-Ung descended to Taebaeksan with a group of three thousand people and established his city. He brought with him the spirit of wind, the spirit of rain, and the spirit of clouds to help him rule. He ruled all matters of wind, rain, and clouds while managing and teaching 360 tasks[39] *of the human world. These included matters of farming, birth, illness and healing, laws and penalties, and good and evil.*

Around this time, a bear[40] *and a tiger*[41] *wanted to become human and came to Hwan-Ung for help. He gave them each a bundle of sacred mugwort*[42] *and 20 pieces of sacred garlic,*[43] *saying, "If you eat only this for 100 days without seeing sunlight, you will receive a human body."*

---

37) Divine son (Suh-ja). A child conceived by a spirit woman (Shin-Nyeo) and a male specially selected for his physical abilities and excellence. Suh-ja are considered special and divine and given their mother's last name. A similar practice can be found in ancient Mesopotamian culture, where the temple of Ishtar referred to the children birthed by Amelu, the temple priestess.

38) While there is no clear record of the three Chunbu-in, they're thought to be the items required to rule the tribe that represented the divine right. Best estimates are that they consisted of a sacred mirror representing the light of sky, a bell or rattle reproducing the sound of the heaven, and a sacred sword representing the role of a sacred priest in both rituals and military positions. These three tools are still the main tools used by Korean shamans.

39) Sam-Il Shingo was the scripture of more than 360 guidelines for the ancient Korean people, written in 366 ancient alphabets. Chamjun Gyegyong is the spiritual text of the ancient Korean people, containing 366 phrases.

40) Thought to be from a bear totem tribe.

41) From a tiger totem tribe.

42) Mugwort is thought to cleanse blood, improve circulation, and offer warming, healing power to a women's womb and reproductive organs, assisting in conception and healthy pregnancies.

43) Garlic is thought to stimulate and invigorate the body. It also has powerful antiseptic powers, can strengthen the immune system, vitalize energy, and enhance stamina.

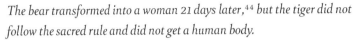

The bear transformed into a woman 21 days later,[44] but the tiger did not follow the sacred rule and did not get a human body.

Ung-Nyeo (Bear Woman) did not have anyone to marry, so she prayed to become pregnant at the sacred altar tree. Hwan-Ung temporarily took on a human form to marry Ung-Nyeo, and together they had a son. He was named Dangun Wanggum.[45]

Dangun established a city near Pyong-yang and named it Joseon.[46] Later he moved the capital to Asadal near Mt. Baekaksan, then eventually returned to Pyong-yang. After Dangun ruled for 1,500 years, the ancient Chinese kingdom of Ju made Gija the official king of Joseon. Dangun went to Asadal and became a Sanshin (mountain god).[47] There were a total of 47 Danguns, and GoJoseon lasted for 1,908 years.

INTERPRETATION

This myth shows that Dangun Wanggum and the kingdom GoJoseon were born through the union of the *Chunshin* tribe (a tribe that worshipped the sky) and the *Gisin* tribe (a tribe that worshipped the earth, such as through animal totems). The culture of worshipping the sky and the land is still retained in Korea today, as shown by the shrines of *Sunghwang-dang*, *Chunwang-dang*, and *Sanshin-dang*.

If Korean Shamanism (*Mu-Gyo* or *Samshin-Gyo*) originated from Mago Samshin, then the second Dangun of GoJoseon, Buru (부루단군), initiated the renaissance of Korean Shamanism during his reign.

---

44) Twenty-one days represents the moon cycle, or a women's menstrual cycle—the ideal duration of time in which to conceive. In this instance, the guidance was to pray inside for 100 days, but the result could also be achieved in one moon cycle of 21 days.

45) The title of Dangun Wanggum (단군왕검) represents both the spiritual leader (Dangun) and the political ruler/king (Wanggum).

46) Dangun's Joseon is now referred as Ancient Joseon (GoJoseon) to distinguish from the Joseon Dynasty (1392-1897 CE) which ruled Korea many years later.

47) The last Dangun, the 47th ruler named Goyeolga who left the kingdom for the mountains on lunar September 9th and is thought to have become a mountain god, or Sanshin.

Chunbu, the Divine Ways, and Samshin Philosophy Explained

THE THREE VIRTUES (삼진): GOODNESS (선), CLEARNESS (청), AND GENEROSITY(후)

Samshin is the unchanging origin of the people and states that Three Virtues exist within humans. Symbolically, the Three Virtues are best reflected through the sun's brightness. Sunlight is good, clear, and generous, and because of this true nature of the sun, all things in the universe live and die. When humans follow these virtues and protect their sanctity, this can also end suffering, disease, and shallowness. Reclaiming a true nature of goodness, clearness, and generosity is a return to the original state—to Mago Samshin.

THE THREE DOOMS (삼망): EVILNESS (악), UNCLEARNESS (탁), AND LACK (박)

Three Dooms weaken the lives of all things in the universe and destroy human nature. Humans enter the womb with only the nature of the Three Virtues, just like the sun, but get them mixed up with the Three

Dooms after birth. People live confused, chaotic lives by exhibiting various combinations of the virtues and dooms. When a doomed nature destroys one's true nature, people lose their humanity and die. Humans can get tangled up in the Three Dooms through bodily temptations and sensations. Since the *Omi* Incident, the sensations of our physical bodies can cause temptations toward evilness, unclearness, and lack. Emotions, energies, and bodily sensations can sometimes influence humans to lie, become greedy, or act hurtfully toward one another.

Humans can protect their innate nature of the Three Virtues by caring for their mind, soul, and body. The first way to do this is to train the mind to recognize and maintain its authentic and original goodness. The second way is to train the soul's energy to stay clear and pure. The third way is to generously nurture and love the body. When one's mind, soul, and body work together to preserve the Three Virtues, their existence becomes the house of Divine Ways—the Three Virtues. Humans then may become the physical manifestation of Samshin in the world.

One can entertain the belief that the three major Asian philosophies—Confucianism, Buddhism, and Taoism—may have originated from the ancient Samshin philosophy.

	BUDDHISM	TAOISM	CONFUCIANISM
FOCUS ON	True Self	Clear Soul/Spirit	Control Energy
PRACTICE OF	Mind	Soul	Body
CONTROLS	Emotions	Breathing	Sensations
PHILOSOPHY	Cut away all feelings and release them and clear the mind to see the original state of mind and reach enlightenment	Use breathing and the power of the spirit within to reach a state of prolonged, age-defying human life, like that of deities and gods	Resist physical desires, control behaviors and actions, and use bodily energy in proper, good ways to reach a state of goodness and honor

The Samshin philosophy believes that three parts make up oneness, as opposed to the binary philosophy of yin and yang. The spiritual foundation of Korean Shamanism originates from the Samshin faith, via the most essential wisdom of *Saeng Saeng Ji Saeng* (생생지생): *that all living things in the universe have value and must be respected accordingly.* The role of Korean shamans should be to practice the Three Virtues themselves while helping more people reclaim these innate virtues and heal from their dooms. This was the original intention of Budo, the Divine City established by Dangun: to benefit the world and people far and wide (재세이화, 홍익인간).

ABOUT *CHUNBU GYEONG* (천부경)

Chunbu Gyeong is a spiritual text that was passed down orally in ancient Korea. It is comprised of nine lines of nine letters each, for a total of 81 letters.

Initially, the first Hwan-Ung, Guhbalhwan (3898–3805 BCE), descended onto the heavenly mountain (Mt. Taebaek) and established a sacred city, ordering a holy scholar named Hyukduk to create and keep the sacred text that was carved into a large boulder in ancient script. Many years later, Gowoon Choi Chiwon (857–? CE) took the script, translated it into Chinese

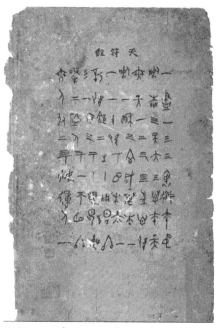

Source: *The Korea History Times*, 2020[48]

characters, and published it into a booklet. Years later, around 1917, the Buddhist monk Gyeyonsu, working in what is today Mt. Myohyansan, shared the text with the world.

48) Oh, Jong-hong. "Unearthed Cheonbugyeong of Janggunbongmaru, Oracle Bone Gate, Baekdusan Mountain." The Korea History Times, 3 Mar. 2020, http://www.koreahiti.com/news/articleView.html?idxno=4000

CHUNBU GYEONG: THE SCRIPTURE OF HEAVENLY WAY

One is the beginning of all and comes from Nothingness.
This One divides into the heavens and sky, earth, and humanity and
   remains limitless.

Arising from One, the heavens are first, the earth is second, human-
   ity is third.
One accumulates to Ten, and Three governs the changes of all things.

Heaven is based on two (yin and yang) and operates by Three,
Earth is based on two and works by Three,
Humanity is based on two works by Three.

The great Three of Heaven, Earth, and Humanity unite into Six,
then give birth to Seven, Eight, and Nine.

Everything moves in accordance with Three and Four;
everything rotates under Five and Seven.

One continues rotating and moving in mysterious and infinite ways,
but the root stays the same. The root is the Mind, which shines radiantly
   like the sun.

Humanity, united with heaven and earth, is the Ultimate One (One in
   the center).

One is the end of all and returns to Nothingness.

APPENDIX 3

The Timeline of Ancient Korean Nations[49]

MAGOSUNG	The beginning of the universe
HWANG-GUNG ERA	Estimated approximately 11,000 years ago
YOO-IN ERA	Years unknown
HWAN-IN ERA	?? to 3897 BCE
HWAN-UNG ERA	**BAEDAL KINGDOM** 3897 BCE–2333 BCE
DANGUN ERA	**GOJOSEON OR ANCIENT JOSEON** 2333 BCE–238 BCE
SAM HAN ERA	the period after GoJoseon and before the Three Kingdom Era

49) For simplicity purpose, excludes various smaller or short-lived ancient kingdoms and confederations not commonly mentioned.

THREE KINGDOM ERA

GOGURYEO KINGDOM	37 BCE–668 CE
BAEKJAE KINGDOM	18 BCE–660 CE
SILLA KINGDOM	57 BCE–935 CE
GAYA CONFEDERATION	42–532 CE

UNIFIED SILLA ERA

SILLA KINGDOM (UNIFIED)	668–935 CE
BALHAE CONFEDERATION	698–926 CE
GORYEO KINGDOM	918–1392 CE
JOSEON KINGDOM	1392–1897 CE
KOREAN EMPIRE	1897–1910 CE
JAPANESE COLONIAL PERIOD	1910–1945 CE

MODERN ERA

NORTH KOREA	1945–present
SOUTH KOREA	1945–present

APPENDIX 4
An Overview of Korean Shamanism

1) CHANGES IN KOREAN SHAMANISM OVER TIME

Humans have likely always felt wonder and amazement towards the universe, nature's phenomena, and her powers—historically, especially when experiencing natural disasters, humans experienced feelings of reverence. This reverence is directly tied to the supernatural—the belief that an absolute power within the universe can be prayed to for needs like comfort and safety. Ancient civilizations believed the sky, earth, sun, moon, stars, mountains, rivers, ocean, trees, and other elements of nature have supernatural and magical powers and started performing rituals to ask for well-being and blessings. In addition to ancient people's reverence for nature and its powers, ritual expression of gratitude also became an important practice. Such rituals are probably the origins of *Gut* (굿), Korean Shamanic rituals.

Ancient rulers monopolized rituals involving the sky, justifying their right to rule by indicating they were the only entities capable of ritualistically communicating with the heavens. In eastern civilizations, when a new kingdom was established or a new emperor was throned, a ritual was performed to announce the beginning to heaven and earth. In early Jewish and Christian traditions, Moses is thought to have received ten commandments after performing a ritual at Mount Sinai, which were then followed by his people because they came after he communicated with god via ritual. Across the ancient world, the right to perform rituals to heaven was an essential power and tool for ruling in early civilizations.

From the beginning of GoJoseon

Korean Shamanism is intertwined with the history of the Korean people. In 2333 BCE, Dangun Wanggum (단군왕검) established Ancient Joseon (GoJoseon) as the civilization's shaman priest as well as its ruler. *Dangun* means "one who performed a ritual to heaven," and *Wanggum* means "one that ruled the land and people."

Unfortunately, there aren't many recorded examples of Korean Shamanic rituals. The oldest written record of our religious traditions can be found in the *Romance of Three Kingdoms*,[50] where the *Yonggo* ritual of the Buyeo Kingdom, the *Dongmaeng* ritual of the Goguryo Kingdom, and the *Muchun* of Ye are mentioned. These rituals to the sky were the foundation of what has become *Gut* today.

Yonggo means "to receive while playing drums," *Dongmaeng* means "to swear and pray to the sun and moon rising from the eastern sky with an offering of animal's blood," and *Muchun* means "to dance toward the sky." They resemble today's Shamanic ritual of *Yilwolsungshin Maji Gut*, the Welcoming of the Celestial God, in which an offering is made to the East through drumming and dancing in order to receive energy and blessings from the sun, moon, and stars.

While there aren't many, we can find a few examples suggesting what such rituals may have looked like in the ancient kingdoms of the Korean people.

---

[50] *Romance of the Three Kingdoms* is a 14th-century Chinese historical novel attributed to Luo Guanzhong.

"...it is a long-haired tail of an ox, the one who dances holds it and shakes it while dancing." [51]

"...the woman is capable of doing unseen shapeless work because she is one who calls gods with dance; she dances wearing a robe with long sleeves." [52]

Shamanic habits of the Goguryeo Kingdom (37 BCE to 668 CE)

In Goguryeo, people believed shamans could guess the illness or disease of a patient, foresee the life of a baby still in the womb, and predict natural disasters. The nation's official shaman was always asked for guidance whenever there was a national hardship.

Some examples of such instances were recorded in the ancient Korean text *Samguk Sagi: The History and Stories of Three Ancient Kingdoms*.

In King Yuri's 19th year (1 CE), during the ritual, the pig reserved as an offering had run away, and two men (Takri and Sabi) captured it and severed its leg nerves to prevent it from running away again. The king was furious and killed the men by throwing them into a hole. Later, the king was ill, and the shaman said the illness was caused by the two dead men's spirits. Once she performed a ritual, he was better.

In King Chadae's 3rd year (148 CE), the shaman spoke of a mystical fox and recommended the king perform good deeds.

In King Sinsang's 13th year (209 CE), the shaman predicted a baby in the womb would become an empress.

In King Dongchun's 8th year (234 CE) after the queen's death, the shaman received divine guidance to plant seven rows of pine trees in front of the queen's grave.

In King Bojang's 4th year (645 CE), in the summer month of May,

---

51) From ancient text of 강희자전, 旄旄牛尾 舞者所持以指麾 (모모우미 무자소지이지휘) This indicates a shaman used an ox's tail to dance with during the ritual.

52) 설문해자, 女能事無形 而舞降神者也 象人兩袂舞形 (여능사무형 이무강신자야 상인양몌무형) This image resembles modern Korean shaman dancing in ceremonial robes in rituals.

the Tang dynasty invaded Korean land, and the king had a shaman perform a ritual at the shrine of Jumong, the ancient founder of Goguryeo.

Shamanic Habits of the Baekje Kingdom (18 BCE–660 CE)

Out of the three ancient kingdoms of Korea, Baekje has the fewest records of Shamanic practices. Considering they shared their origins with the kingdom of Goguryeo, one can guess they had similar cultures and rituals. In *Samguk Sagi*, there is mention that during King Onjo's 25th year, when the well at the palace was overflowing, and a two-headed cow was born, "Sun Wiseman" was consulted—this person was probably a shaman.

Shamanic Habits of the Silla Kingdom (57 BCE–935 CE)

The kingdom of Silla seemed to have the most robust Korean Shamanic practices, based on ancient records. In the Silla dialect, they called shamans *Chachaung* (차차웅); here, *Ung* probably came from the ancient ancestor of Hwan-Ung, mentioned throughout *Budoji*, particularly in Chapter 11.

Out of the three ancient kingdoms, Silla accepted the Buddhist religion last and only deemed it a national religion after a Buddhist monk's martyrdom. This was at least 155 years later than in Goguryeo and Baekje. This indicates the Silla people's beliefs in Shamanism were much stronger.

In the Silla dialect, language referencing kings reflected the old term for a ritual priest, and the famous gold crown worn by the Silla king was worn when they led rituals. There is a well-known old tale about Silla's famous general, Kim Yushin, who slays his beloved white horse after taking him to visit a woman called Heavenly Mistress. During this visit, he ends his relationship with her to be more loyal to the queen. This woman was likely to be one of spiritual or divine order—a *mudang* or shaman. This tale demonstrates how Silla's leadership was transitioning from following Shamanism to Buddhism around this time.

Once Buddhism began proliferating through Goguryeo, Baekje, and

Silla, the kings' most important focus was strengthening their ruling powers. Using Buddhism as the national religion to reinforce their powers meant Shamanism was pushed out from the leadership. There are many mystical stories of the supernatural powers of Buddhist monks in *Samguk Sagi* and *Samguk Yusa*, but these myths have likely been edited from old Shamanic stories of the shaman's abilities.

Shamanic Habits of the Goryeo Kingdom (918–1392 CE)

During the Goryeo dynasty, Shamanic practices were combined with Taoism and used widely inside the palace and among laypeople. According to *Goryeosa Ohengji*, there are many records of shamans performing rituals for rain.

1021 King Hyunjong: *In May, there was drought, and a gathering of shamans prayed for rain.*

1101 King Sukjong and 1162 King Yejong: *In May, shamans gathered to perform a rain ritual.*

1133 King Injong: *In May, female shamans gathered with 300 people at the ritual office and conducted a rain ritual.*

1134 King Injong: *In June, 250 shamans gathered at the capital to perform a rain ritual.*

1173 King Myungjong: *In April, shamans gathered in Byunja and performed a rain ritual.*

1250 King Gojong: *Shamans conducted a rain ritual.*

1284, 1289, 1304, 1306 King Chungryul: *Due to drought, the market was relocated, and there shamans performed a rain ritual.*

By the era of the Goryeo Kingdom, the shamans' societal power as the nation's elders and wisdom teachers had transferred to Buddhist monks, and the shamans only performed rituals for rain and other business, as needed.

In Goryeo's old folk culture, when people became ill, they worshipped spirits and fought illness using divination and magic instead of medicine. This indicates that Shamanic practices were widely practiced during the Goryeo Dynasty. From the time of ancient GoJoseon, shamans worked as healers and medicine women, and this work continued too. There is also mention of some shamans practicing unethically, using divination and curses to harm people or using trickery to influence people.

According to *Goryeosa (History of Goryeo)*, many *mudangs* came in and out of the palace to give advice or conduct divination rituals. From 1178 to 1217, they also had a temporary office inside the palace called *Byeolgieun,* where their role was to pray for the peace and well-being of the nation.

According to the same text, people of any status (noble, layperson, or slave) could become a *mudang.* If an upper-class or noblewoman became a shaman, they were called *Sunkwan* (선관). If a lower-class or laywoman became a shaman, they were called *mudang* (무당). *Sunkwans* had an official position to pray and perform rituals for the royal family's well-being and blessing.

During the reign of King Choongsuk, the sister of a significant official of the left chair became a *mudang,* and she was called *Sunkwan* and worked at Songak temple.

The start of the oppression of shamans and Shamanic practices in the Goryeo Kingdoms is also recorded.

According to the ancient text of *Dongguktongam,* in 1131 (CE), the king declared Shamanism an unethical, dark practice and ordered shamans to be removed outside of the capital city. From then on, shamans were not allowed to enter the four gates of the capital. However, even during this oppression, the palace and royal family still used shamans' services for rituals such as the *Palgwanhwe* festival—the palace's largest celebration ritual.

Goryeosa (History of Goryeo) also shows that there was a profession of healing diseases using divination. The position of Divination Healer became officially recognized. The Goryeo Kingdom continued this practice, requiring people to pass an exam to be selected for the position. The Divination Healer belonged to the office of medicine and healing, and their role was that of a high-ranking official.

Shamanic Practices during the Joseon Kingdom (1392–1910 CE)

From the original shaman-king (*Dangun Wanggum*) system of ancient Korea, each of the kingdoms that followed utilized Buddhism as the national religion to strengthen their ruling power, pushing Shamanism outside its once-central role. But once Confucianism entered the country, Shamanism was oppressed as "an obscene form of spirituality."

Especially during the Joseon Dynasty, shamans became among the eight lowest-class people, alongside slaves, butchers, street performers, artisans, courtesans, pallbearers, and Buddhist monks. *Mudang*s and Buddhist monks were classified as the lowest class of people and endured discrimination and oppression in the nation's effort to reduce the people's reliance on Shamanism and Buddhism.

But while the government suppressed Shamanism, they could not eliminate the folk indigenous faith and the dependence people had on it. Though politically oppressed, people still practiced Shamanism, and even the royal family and members of the higher-up *Yangban* class often relied on the services of shamans. During the Joseon Kingdom, even the political agenda to promote Confucianism and reject Buddhism and Shamanism couldn't entirely sever the people's connection to their ancient practices— when the service of a shaman was needed, they were called upon.

Some records note that in 1413, King Taejong employed shamans to perform a rain ritual. Earlier, in 1392, a shaman predicted the king's fall from the horse. In 1418, there is a record stating that in February, there was a complaint that a palace shaman, Gayi, was unable to heal the illness of a royal family member and called for her to be punished. In King Sejong's time, in June of 1420, the king was ill, and the empress ordered a shaman to conduct a healing prayer ritual.

1515 King Joongjong: *In April, the official shaman named Dolbi visited the palace often to perform rituals removing curses, preventing disasters, and welcoming blessings. In doing so, she received gifts of money and clothes from the king and returned home.*

1575 King Sunjo: *When the empress was ill, the shaman conducted a healing prayer at her sickbed.*

Until 1525, the Joseon Kingdom maintained an office of Celestial Business where the official shaman could pray for the royal family's well-being and ask for blessings. When there was a bad drought, the palace would gather hundreds of shamans to perform a rain ritual. A smaller office was also established where shamans could conduct healing work for village people, similar to today's free clinics. This form of a lay-person's clinic employed shamans and medicinal doctors to heal people.

To further oppress Shamanism, Joseon kept updated records of the names of all *mudang*s and collected taxes. They imposed high taxes on the shamans and used the money to bolster the kingdom's wealth and military. Sometimes they would assign a village shaman, and taxes would be forgiven if she could keep the villagers healthy and peaceful. Some argued that collecting taxes from shamans meant the government recognized their role as professionals. Still, because their taxes benefited government operations, Korea only ended taxes for shamans in 1895 as part of a modernization effort.

Shamanism During and After Japanese Colonization

During the Japanese colonization period (1910–1945 CE), the ruling powers declared that only Shintoism, Buddhism, and Christianity be considered religions while classifying all other traditions within "similar groups." Once again, Shamanism was suppressed, and its practitioners abused and oppressed. Around this westernized modernization period (1930s), the elites of Joseon were even harsher than the Japanese in deeming Shamanism a superstition, and they led the oppression effort of Shamanism. During this time, there were many crackdowns toward ending village Shamanic rituals, which had long served as powerful ways for villagers to reduce conflict and forge connections. Many village shrines and sacred ritual sites were destroyed during this time.

After independence from Japan and during the American occupation, Christianity was widely disseminated and deemed Shamanism evil and devil-worshipping. Shamanism continued to suffer.

In the 1970s, with the New Village Movement, the Korean government officially launched a campaign called "Kill Superstition." This was a pro-Christianity political effort to destroy any remaining village shrines and guardian posts. During this time, most of the remaining village rituals disappeared.

The Importance of Preserving Shamanic Principles in Today's Modern World

In ancient times, Korea's people regarded spirits as wise entities, and they worshipped and listened to the guidance of the spirits. Korean shamans usually served nature spirits and ancestor spirits. The nature gods were the Sky god, the Land god, the Water god, and others, while the ancestor gods were historical heroes who died unfairly, as well as the actual shaman's personal ancestors. *Gut* (ritual) performed prayers and offerings to the *shin* (신, gods and deities) or to *gwi* (귀, spirits of the dead).

Gut is performed by the priestess of Shamanism, orienting the *mudang* or shaman toward heaven. *Gut* remains a part of people's lives by supporting their personal lives, the well-being of their village, and the entire nation's well-being and abundance. And through *Gut*, the principle of Korean Shamanism called *"Saeng Saeng Ji Saeng"* (생생지생)—meaning *all things with life in the universe have worth and value and need respect*—is passed on. Instead of the dual balancing of yin and yang, this offers a three-element balancing that elevates the need for harmony and unity. In yin and yang, only two entities need to come into agreement. However, with the Shamanic principle of *Saeng Saeng Ji Saeng*, an agreement between two entities must also benefit, or at least not harm, a third party. Korean Shamanism attributes magical divinity to all things in nature to honor this principle of respect. This is why *mudangs* were also called *manshin* (만신), meaning 10,000 spirits, because they honor and worship many spirits.

With the shared intention and wish for the common good inherent in *Gut*, the ritual allows people to heal and cheer one another to become happier; it has the power to release the oppressed hearts of people and resolve conflicts among them. Because *Gut* has the nature of a festival and celebration, as well as other spiritual purposes, it becomes a container in which people can unite in community and harmony.

The performance of *Gut* is specifically scheduled on an auspicious day, as determined by considering astronomy and other factors—the day *Gut* is performed is always a good one. While *Gut* performances can look slightly different based on their region, the overarching purpose is consistent. *Gut* is the Korean people's political, economic, historical, spiritual, philosophical, and cultural expression, representing the country's core authentic being.

With the globalization of Korean pop culture, Koreans cannot forget their core beliefs and nature and must look at the world with clear eyes instead of assessing their beliefs, practices, and culture through the lens of the outside world.

According to the Korean folk religion dictionary, Korean Shamanism is a religion that seeks to improve and benefit the present human life, so even today, it is a spiritual tradition that has an impact on human lives. Rather than dogma and ideological benefit, or afterlife salvation and the manifestation of a philosophical vision, Korean Shamanism offers practical, tangible benefits: helping regular people discover wisdom from within themselves, the surrounding nature, and other people to support their navigation of real-life challenges.

2) DIFFERENCES IN KOREAN *MUDANG*S

Korean shamans, *mudangs* (무당), are categorized mainly as either *Seseup-mu* (세습무) or *Gangshin-mu* (강신무).

Seseup-mu shamans

Seseup-mu are shamans who learn the rites, rituals, and practices from their parents and follow an ancestral tradition of Korean Shamanic arts and performances. Usually, everyone in the family would be employed in some form of Shamanic work.

While these shamans worship their gods and perform rituals, they don't go through the process of receiving gods or of possession by spirits during a practice. They don't have a shrine for their gods, nor do they give psychic readings (*gongsu*, 공수, spirits' words) during rituals. Overall, they do not have the essential element of *Gangshin-mu*, which is the ability to receive spirits and communicate with them. These hereditary shamans inherit their position as a lifetime career, and they learn the specific rituals, songs, dances, and instruments of their family's Shamanic traditions.

Some examples of *Seseup-mu* are the *Dangoleh* (당골레) of Jeolla province, the *Mudang Jimosani* (지모사니) of Gyeongsang province, the *Shimbang* (심방) of Jeju, and the *Sani* (사니) of Gyeonggi province. The female shamans mainly utilize song and dance in their practice, while the male shamans usually play musical instruments for the rituals. Women who marry into these shaman families learn the Shamanic rites, songs, and dances from their in-laws. The daughters of these families learn how to perform these rites from a young age by following their parents. Sons learn how to play the musical instruments and Shamanic songs from a young age as well and often become experts in other traditional Korean musical arts such as *Pansori* and traditional instruments. In the *Seseup-mu* lineage, if one or both parents are shamans, all the children will also become shamans. This means that shaman blood runs through the family, referred to as "having a root."

During the Joseon dynasty, shamans were considered to be of the lowest class, and the area where they performed business was *Dangolpan*. These are primarily found in the southern part of Korea, spreading out from the Han River, but today, there aren't many known or active shamans of these types. Those that do remain are around the coasts: the East Sea *Byeolshin Gut*, the South Sea *Byeolshin Gut*, the Jindo *Ssitkimgut*, the Shinahn *Honmaji Gut*, the Goheung *Ssitkimgut,* and the main village ritual of Gyeonggi province.

In the past, people born into a shaman family weren't allowed to marry people outside of their own class. They had to marry within their professions and weren't allowed to change those professions later. To be a shaman was a lifetime career.

But in the modernized Korea, many shamans were able to leave the family profession. Because their only job was to perform Shamanic songs and dance rituals, they contributed to the development of traditional art, and some have become recognized as famous singers and performers.

Gangshin-mu shamans

*Gangshin-mu mudang*s are considerably different from *Seseup-mu*. *Gangshin-mu* receive spirits in their bodies to speak *gongsu*, making them shamans that experience possession and ecstasy. These shamans go through the "spirit sickness" (*shin-byung*, 신병) and maintain shrines (*shin-dang*, 신당) for performing rituals for their gods.

The main elements of a *Gangshin-mu* shaman practice are spirit sickness, maintaining a shrine, and performing psychic readings and rituals. These four practices are required to be considered a *Gangshin-mu* shaman. The spirit illness of *mu-byung* (무병) or *shin-byung* (신병) is a common experience of *Gangshin-mu* Shamanism; a mental or physical illness—often a hardship—one endures before becoming a shaman. These experiences, similar to a spiritual possession, tend to originate at birth and become stronger as the future shaman ages. The only way to become free from this "spirit illness" is to be initiated into Shamanism.

Often, the spirit illness is described as "possessed by spirits," "ghosts are on her," or "spirits picked her." Those with spirit illness exhibit strange behaviors and confused mental states, as possessing spirit interrupts their normal life rhythm. There is no cure for "spirit illness" in modern allopathic medical practices.

The symptoms of spirit illness vary for different people. Some exhibit similar symptoms to one suffering from multiple personality disorder, performing strange behaviors, or describing the experience of surreal phenomena. Others exhibit serious physical illnesses with unknown causes, such as physical weakness, an inability to eat, extreme weight loss, heavy uterine bleeding, and even bodily paralysis. Many describe experiencing premonitions and prophecies, displaying psychic gifts and insights.

When those chosen by spirits don't accept the spirits, they suffer consequences. These are called *Shin-bul* (신벌, spirit punishments), and they vary widely—anything from the dismantling of a family or marriage to economic loss and other misfortunes. The most drastic and violent consequence is called *Indari* (인다리, human bridge), in which one's family members die, one by one, building a bridge of corpses.

When we look at the process by which the *Gangshin-mu* becomes a *mudang*, it becomes clear that after suffering from spirit sickness, they meet their spirit mother *mudang* and perform *Naerim-gut* (내림굿, initiation ritual), receiving and serving the gods, finally embarking on the journey toward becoming a *mudang*. There are three types of initiation rituals a future *Gangshin-mu* shaman must undergo—the *Heoju-gut* (허주굿), *Naerim-gut* (내림굿), and *Soseul-gut* (솟을굿). *Heoju-gut* is the ceremony of clearing evil or unnecessary spirits, *Naerim-gut* is the ceremony of receiving the gods who descend to work with the *mudang*, and *Soseul-gut* is the ceremony that activates and energizes the gods who help the shaman do their work successfully.

During initiation, their spirit mother (a more experienced *mudang* mentor) helps seat the gods at the altar, soothing them while asking the initiate to find hidden Shamanic tools to confirm their spiritual connection. In a tradition called *Gu-up* (구업), an old shaman would bury their Shamanic tools in the ground before dying, and the future shaman, while possessed by spirits, is instructed to find and dig up these buried tools. Those successful at *gu-up* were thought to be especially powerful and gifted.

Most *Gangshin-mu mudang*s are cured of spirit sickness after their initiation ritual and thus begin their shaman work. They also start giving readings by inviting and embodying one of the gods received during their ceremony.

Once the *mudang* has received the initiation rite, she succeeds her spirit mother's work as a student. Those supervising and performing the initiation ritual as spirit mother and spirit father are usually highly experienced and advanced in age. They form a relationship with the newly initiated *mudang*, who begins their own work as their mentors' spirit daughter or son (also called spirit baby or student). These relationships are meant to last a lifetime, starting from the day of the *Naerim-gut*.

The newly initiated *Gangshin-mu* shaman follows their spirit mother, performing *Guts* and learning the rites, dances, Shamanic narrative songs, psychic readings, and more along the way. They learn how to prepare an offering table, prepare and cook traditional ritual foods, and other knowledge necessary to perform a *Gut*.

The basic services offered by the new *Gangshin-mu* are psychic readings (called *shin-jeom* 신점, or "god divination" because they are thought to rely entirely on the energy of their gods), *gosa* blessings, and various other Shamanic rituals (*Gut*). They also predict the future in multiple ways, such as writing channeled text, tossing brass coins, and scattering rice grains.

During *Gut* rituals, the shaman uses traditional percussion instruments and performs a dance of jumps and spins, signifying the embodiment of spirit energy. Then she provides *gongsu*, completely immersed in the spirit possession, channeling them. The shaman often wears magnificently colorful costumes designed to display the power of their gods.

Other than the two types of *mudang*s, there is the *Beop-sa* (법사), who is not a shaman but participates in the Shamanist ceremony by chanting the sutras. Originally, the term *Beop-sa* referred to the Buddhist monk who devoted themselves to self-discipline, giving sermons, and living as a model for the world. Through the influence of Buddhism assimilating with Korean Shamanism, the term gradually came to include those who read ancient sutras and prayers.

It is possible to become a *Beop-sa* through an experience similar to *Gangshin-mu*—by receiving spirits in the body. One can also become *Beop-sa* by learning from a teacher. The training includes free recitation of various sutras to the beat of percussion instruments and the production of prayers and chants needed for rituals.

Today, most practitioners become a *Beop-sa* through study rather than spirit possession. While there are similarities between the activities of *mudang* and *Beop-sa,* their differences are apparent regarding spirit illness or possession. Unlike *mudang*, who invites and appeases the spirits and gods to heal spirit illness, the *Beop-sa* attempts to heal the spirit sickness by catching and trapping the spirits.

Beop-sa were especially effective at performing exorcism rituals and often traveled across the country to do their work. They were also asked to help with birth chart reading, choosing auspicious dates, naming children, feng shui, and selecting gravesites.

Because they used the narration of various sutras in their work, they spent a lot of time studying the ancient texts and prayers. Their work continues today by men near Chungcheong province and Gangwon province.

3) SHAMANIC RITUAL PRACTICES (*GUT*, 굿) & THEIR SIGNIFICANCE

The Korean Shamanic rite of *Gut* takes a variety of forms, each with its own purpose and in consideration of the request of the designated person. The following rituals are the most essential and the most common.

Jaesu-gut (재수굿, Fortune Rituals)

The *Jaesu-gut* prays for a household's peace, stability, and financial success, as well as the prosperity of offspring, longevity, and good fortune for the family. When performed at the start of the new year, the *Gut* prays for good luck in the new year. It is also performed in October, the tenth month of the lunar year, when a new harvest is offered to the gods and ancestors—most often to the house gods responsible for the family's well-being.

The *Jaesu-gut* is also called *Cheonshinmaji* (천신맞이, receiving of celestial gods), *Gyeongsa-gut* (경사굿, celebration ritual), and *Antaek-gut* (안택굿, peace and well-being ritual).

Jaesu-gut is usually performed at the beginning of the year or in the spring or fall. The dates are chosen based on the family member's birth charts and astrology. It is customary to perform this ritual annually or every three years, but it can also be conducted in exceptional circumstances, such as if misfortune befalls a household.

Jinogi-gut (진오기굿, Rituals for the Dead)

As a *Gut* for consoling the deceased and guiding them to the otherworld peacefully, *Jinogi-gut* is referred to by different names in each region of Korea. It is called *Jinogi-gut* in Seoul region, *Suwang-gut* (수왕굿) in Hwanghae province, *Dari-gut* (다리굿) in Pyungan province, *Mangmuk-gut* (망묵굿) in Hamgyeong province, *Ogwi-gut* (오귀굿) in Gyeongsang province, and *Ssitkim-gut* (씻김굿) in Jeolla province.

Death is a sorrowful and solemn matter for anyone, but in Korean Shamanism, unlike in Buddhism, it has a festive character. The comfort and repose found in the consciousness of death is worthwhile to the deceased and provides comfort and hope to those who remain living. In this sense, death is not seen as an end but rather a new birth, reflecting the view that death is not just a sad thing. The concept of death as a celebration is well-developed in Shamanism.

Rites for consoling the deceased, like *Jinogi-gut,* reflect the idea of sending off the souls of the dead to the afterlife or paradise. Rites are usually conducted as early as 49 days after death or as late as within two to three years, as requested of a shaman. It is believed that not performing this ritual could cause the soul of the dead to bring illness or harm to the family or its descendants, but conducting the ritual allows the spirit to help the family as an ancestral guardian.

Whether the deceased's soul brings blessings or harm to the family is not a fixed matter, but it depends on the deceased's relationship with them while living. The Shamanic *Gut* shatters the emotional wall—any harmful elements threatening to sever positive relationships between the living and the dead—and facilitates the dissolution of resentments to promote peaceful coexistence. More about Korean indigenous beliefs about death and the afterlife are discussed in the later section of this appendix.

Naerim-gut (내림굿, Shamanic Initiation Ritual)

This *Gut,* in which one who suffers from the spirit sickness receives their gods as a shaman-to-be, is also called *shin-gut* (신굿) or *shinmyeong-gut* (신명굿). As a requisite rite for becoming a *mudang,* it turns one into a priestess aligned with divine intentions. It's possible to view *Naerim-gut* as the process of becoming a *mudang* who then guides others to discover their own nature.

Traditionally there were three phases in the *Naerim-gut* ritual; *Heoteun-gut* (허튼굿), *Naerim-gut* (내림굿), and *Soseul-gut* (솟을굿).

Naerim-gut used to be performed after conducting the *Heoteun-gut,* which cleared away evil spirits that may have been accompanying the initiate. Today, these two rituals are combined into one *Naerim-gut,* where an experienced *mudang* clears away bad spirits and then invites in spirit guides and gods for the newly initiated *mudang*.

The procedure of this *Gut* varies by region and takes place in different forms across the country. In most rituals, after dancing, the initiate enters spirit possession and starts to shake their body. It is at this moment that they come to serve *momju-shin* (몸주신), the main gods offering their spiritual power for Shamanic work, which they will serve and work with for their lifetime. Upon receiving the gods, they start offering predictions and live readings to those present at the ritual. This process of giving *gongsu* (공수) is described as "opening the gate of their words."

Long ago, before their rituals, the initiate spent a few days visiting 99 homes in their village, announcing their presence and providing *gongsu*. This tradition was called *geon-rip* (건립), and there were several reasons for this step.

The first was to spread the word. By visiting 99 homes, the *mudang* could advertise her services and establish herself far and wide through the word-of-mouth transfer of the news of their upcoming initiation as a *mudang*.

The second was that through *geon-rip*, the new *mudang* could showcase their Shamanic abilities and magic while overcoming any shame or shyness, as well as any societal prejudice or contempt people had toward *mudang*. It enabled one to become more confident and proud of their calling.

The third was to collect offerings of rice, grains, candles, brassware, drums, or money that neighbors offered the future shaman. Such offerings represented wishes and encouragement from the village people whom the initiate would soon serve as a *mudang*. These offerings also eased the cost of making *Naerim-gut* ritual offerings. In these offerings, the initiate never accepted any ceramics or breakable items because they were thought to be bad luck. Some of the brassware collected was used to make their Shamanic rattle and tools.

Byeong-gut (병굿, Illness Rituals)

Byeong-gut, also called *Woohwan-gut* (우환굿), is performed when there is misfortune in a household. It is used not only for treating sudden illnesses but also any household misfortune, for instance, in a home with frequent minor illnesses and generally unwell people. The character of the *Gut* can be categorized according to the cause of the illness.

In Korean Shamanism, it is believed that all sickness comes from the mischief of spirits. *Byeong-gut* can bring psychological stability to the sufferer of an illness, their family, and others. The identity of the ghost determines the approach to *Byeong-gut*. For example, when an illness comes from one's ancestors, the ritual is performed to serve and appease the ancestors. When an illness is caused by someone who died unmarried, the ritual attempts to marry the soul. When one dies from drowning, a ritual of gathering and collecting the soul from the water is performed. If the illness arises from a grave or the condition of an ancestor's corpse, a ritual to ease the spirit in the grave is performed. Illness due to evil spirits is treated by simply intimidating the ghost and chiding them away.

Most exorcism or *salpuri* (살풀이, clearing of curse or evil) involves this rite, threatening the ghost with cooked millet and kitchen knives. The Shamanic god invoked in these rituals is usually the one considered to be the most powerful in defeating and trapping ghosts, such as Jang Gun (장군, Warrior General god) or Shin Jang (신장, Guardian god).

There are many strategies for chasing away or trapping ghosts during *Byeong-gut* that have been passed down. During the late Joseon period and the Japanese colonial era, the following techniques were used by shamans and ordinary people alike.

1. Beating

This method defeats the ghost by inflicting a physical beating. In this case, the patient's body is directly struck, and by causing severe suffering, it is thought that the ghost occupying the patient's body will not be able to bear the pain and eventually leave, curing that patient of the illness. The beating must not be done by hand but instead with peach or mulberry tree branches that were reaching towards the East. This type of exorcism was used in other religions, such as Protestant churches, and has resulted in occasions when patients were killed.

2. Shocking or Intimidation
This method seeks to shock the ghost by surprising the patient. The illness is thought to be treated with threat and coercion to defeat the spirit and prevent further invasion.

3. Fire and Smoke
Sometimes seen in Korean dramas featuring Shamanism, this method comes from the belief that because fire is yang and the ghost is yin, the spirit can be defeated through fire. The ghost is chased away by burning its entrusted goods or through immersion in smoke.

4. Wounding
This method involves puncturing the patient's body or affected area, causing a bleeding wound on the skin. However, when the face and other vital areas of the body are at risk, a doll or scarecrow is used instead.

5. Binding
This method ties up the ghost causing illness and calamity, and makes it impossible for the spirit to demonstrate its power.

6. Offerings
Unlike other methods of a direct attack on the ghosts, this method politely obeys and appeases the spirit by asking for forgiveness using offerings and gifts. One example of such a technique in Korean Shamanism is a ritual to Smallpox gods.

7. Respect and Obedience
This method involves revering and listening to the ghost, trying not to offend it, and showing respect to earn its sympathy or favor to avoid calamity.

8. *Bujeok* (부적, Talisman)

In this procedure, a talisman made of pictures or letters is sealed with prayerful energy to block the invasion of evil spirits and ward off disease. These *bujeok*s are usually posted on the door. Some people also burn the talisman and drink the ash mixed with salt water.

9. Multiplying Power

This is a method of borrowing the power of another being, not one's own. Often it includes combining the powers of multiple entities to strengthen one's overall abilities. For example, to treat smallpox, a family would borrow a small amount of white rice from ten different households and feed the patient a rice cake made from the offerings. They believed this combined energy would heal the disease.

10. Food or Plant Medicine

This method involves feeding the patient food believed to be filled with energies that will chase the evil spirits away. Sour and spicy flavors are most often used because they are pungent, highly stimulating, and therefore believed to be hated by spirits. For example, in the Hwanghae Province, when treating rabies, it is thought to be good to feed the patient the burnt fur of the dog that transmitted the disease.

11. Balancing Ancestral Graves

In feng shui, it is believed that the destiny of one's descendants is determined mainly by the ancestral remains and the condition of the grave where they are buried. Whether the grave is in good or bad condition depends upon whether it can gain strength from the land. Thus, this method attempts to receive the healing power of the land by arranging graves to strengthen the ancestors. This method is often used by Korean shamans who see the cause of diseases as related to ancestral graves. By correcting the balance of ancestral graves, they attempt to heal illnesses or calamities.

12. Appealing to the Five Senses

This method utilizes the senses of sight (specifically, color), sound, smell, taste, and touch to eradicate a spirit. Typically, ghosts are believed to loathe the colors red and yellow; drumming and metallic sounds or sorrowful exclamations; potent scents; highly spicy, sour, and salty foods; and hot or otherwise painful sensations.

13. Trapping and Blocking

This method attempts to trap the evil spirit within an object, containing it and restricting its movement. Sometimes shamans are invited to chant prayers before trapping the spirit in a piece of white paper and locking it inside a jar or bottle. After the container is sealed tightly, it is buried at a crossroads.

As demonstrated by many different folk healing methodologies, Illness *Gut* is the critical indicator that shamans played the role of healer and doctor in the eras before modern medicine. Even still, in today's age of science and allopathic medicine, there continue to be illnesses treated through *Byeong-gut*.

Shinsa-maji (신사맞이, Receiving Spirit-Work Ritual)

This ritual is carried out by the *mudang*, who serve their own gods by making offerings and expressing gratitude for the gods' guidance and teachings. It also attempts to atone for any mistakes or wrongs the shamans have committed in their work. It is also a time for renewing one's determination and resolution as a shaman priestess; reflecting upon one's devotion to the responsibility of a *mudang*; and finally, considering how one has lived their life thus far.

Through this *Gut*, the *mudang* also expresses thanks to the clients and communities who trust them, wishing each household health and happiness. There are many different names for such rituals, which are performed annually or every three years.

Gosa (고사, Blessing Ritual)

Gosa started as the core household ceremony of offering wishes to the household spirits for a family's well-being. *Gosa* was performed either around the lunar new year (*Seollal*, 설날) or around the fall harvest festival (*Chuseok*, 추석).

In ancient times, families chose an auspicious date to conduct the ritual. Then, they hung a golden thread on their front gate and lay yellow ochre dirt outside as a means of cleansing and protecting. Before the ritual, family members stayed home, limiting exposure to corrupted energies or activities. Traditional offerings usually consisted of dried pollack, skeins, pig's head, rice cakes, and alcohol, though it varied by locality.

Even in today's world of technology and satellites, the ceremony of *Gosa* continues to be popular, carried out by Koreans across socioeconomic class, time, and place. It has become a part of Korean culture, a rite of passage essential to modern activities like launching one's own business, introducing a new high-tech machine, or purchasing a car.

Gosa is not viewed as a superstition particular to a specific group or religion but rather a common ritual performed for one's own comfort. Nowadays, there are frequent instances of *Gosa* being performed before the opening ceremony of a professional sports game to wish the players safety from injury and a good score. In anticipation of the 2002 World Cup, for example, Guus Hiddink, the coach of South Korea's soccer team, carried out *Gosa* for this very purpose.

Gosa represents ancestors' beliefs in perceiving one's household as a universe, where energies of metaphysics and physics work together for all household members. Modern constructions, like new high-rise apartments or Western-style homes, have become a significant reason for eliminating sacred spaces and spiritual culture in individual homes.

4) GODS IN KOREAN SHAMANISM

Korean *mudangs* serve a variety of gods, such as celestial gods, earth or land-based gods, and personal ancestral gods. The following are some of the most common.

1. Samshin (삼신, Triple Goddess)

Samshin is responsible for fertility, pregnancy, childbirth, and the health of the mother and the newborn. Her main power is to bless one with a child, but she also controls the child's health and lifespan, the mother's health after childbirth, and the family's well-being.

Samshin, Image from Sungje Cho's private collection

According to the *Budoji*, Samshin is a trinity of Mago and her two daughters, Gung-hee and So-hee. Regarded as a single feminine deity, she is called Samshin Halmoni (삼신 할머니, Samshin Grandmother), Samshin Sangjae (삼신 상제, Samshin Priestess), Samshin Jesuk (삼신 제석, Samshin Buddha), as well as others.

In Korea, lunar March 3rd is called *Samjitnal* (삼짇날), also the day of Samshin Halmoni.

The belief that Samshin must bless humans with life—the gift of creation—is a part of the indigenous belief that the universe also comes from Samshin. That is because Samshin is the god who created the universe and all things in the universe. This is equivalent to saying that Samshin is the one who made the first human being.

Until a child is ten years old, their life, health, any danger they face, all other good or bad occurrences—every aspect of their life—depends on Samshin. Women seeking fertility used to and continue to visit a shaman to receive the blessing of Samshin.

2. Chilsungshin (칠성신, Seven Star God)

Chilsungshin, Image from Sungje Cho's private collection

Chilsungshin is a god that Koreans have believed in for all of history, alongside Samshin. *Chilsung*, seven stars, deified the Big Dipper, and people believed their fortunes, misfortunes, living and dying all came from this constellation. The Shamanic ritual for Chilsungshin is considered one of the most prominent—partly because it is believed one can see *Chilsung* throughout nature: in springs, wells, mountains, oceans, and more. Chilsungshin is related to water because the ancestors believed the water originated from the Big Dipper. Some older traditional wells were designed as a ladle—a nod to the Big Dipper. Mention of Chilsungshin can often inspire the image of a grandmother praying for her descendants by making an offering of a bowl of clear water drawn at daybreak.

3. Sanshin (산신, Mountain God)

Sanshin, Image from Sungje Cho's private collection

The god who oversees and protects mountains, Sanshin, is considered either male or female, depending on the region. It is said most ancient Sanshin deities were in feminine form, but during the Joseon dynasty, Confucianism gradually influenced their change to male forms. Because Korea's geography has many mountains, it has long observed a culture of mountain worship. In a mountain-worshipping culture, mountains are the center of the universe. Korea's founding myth of Dangun states that his father, Hwan-Ung, descended upon Mt. Taebaeksan, which was believed to be the center of the world. In the ancient text of *Dong Yi Jeon* (동이전, *Record of*

Dong Yi Tribe), it is written that the tribe "respected the mountains and per-formed rituals to the tigers and believed them to be gods." Sanshin worship is connected to the myth of state-building in antiquity. In this light, moun-tain worship is central to Korea's indigenous faith.

Sanshin faith involved believing Sanshin was the protector of the state and performing rituals and rites. This tradition was continued inter-mittently from the Goryeo to Joseon dynasties. Whenever there was a natural disaster, the emperor of Goryeo went to a sacred mountain and performed rites there. During the Joseon Dynasty, Sanshin faith diver-sified, proliferating from the center of national, collective worship to individual and village-based faith. The mountain spirit rites and tradi-tions were organized and managed at local and regional levels instead of national ones.

In every village, there were shrines to the mountain god called *san-shindang* (산신당, Shrine of Mountain God), *sanwangdang* (산왕당, Shrine of Mountain King,) and others. These mountains with shrines were called *dang-san* (당산) and are considered sacred. Over time, shrines at higher altitudes were relocated lower on the mountainside, closer to the villages. This relocation is believed to strengthen the individual faith of the one praying so that the Sanshin will bring the village an abundant harvest, well-being, offspring, or healing.

The body of the Sanshin typically takes the form of a tiger or a sacred divine man with a white beard and robe. The believed connection between tigers and the mountain spirit is found in various ancient texts, in which tigers were also called mountain spirits, mountain guardians, or mountain gods—because the tiger is a powerful, courageous animal, and people believed them to have divine powers. For this reason, brides in wedding ceremonies lay a tiger skin on their carriages as a form of protection, and grooms held a tiger glass as a talisman. Government officials believed owning tiger skin would repel spirits and ghosts that bring bad luck.

Such a belief reveals the idea that ill fortune can be entirely thwarted by the strength of the tigers dominating the mountains of the Korean peninsula. Fear of the tiger and awe of its powerful force led to the tiger being recognized as a sacred entity. In this way, the tiger came to be recognized in the mountainous region as Sanshin, or a spiritual being who assists Sanshin and a guardian spirit of the village, subject to worship.

4. Yongwangshin (용왕신, God of Sea or Water)

The god who presides over water is called Yongwang. At the seaside, people worship this divinity for peace in the household, good health and longevity of family members, a plentiful harvest, bountiful fishing, and safe passage. Of the ceremonies devoted to Yongwang, the most representative is Yongwang *Meogigi* (용왕먹이기, Feeding of Yongwang Ritual).

Yongwang, Image from Sungje Cho's private collection

Typically, Yongwang rituals take place on the first full moon of the lunar new year. There are also occasions when they are performed on other predetermined dates. On Jeju Island, the ceremony most often takes place in lunar February.

Yongwang ritual is performed at various levels among ordinary people. The primary one is the village ritual. At the beginning of January, fishing villages carry out a ritual to pray for a bountiful catch and peace for the fishery in the new year. The tradition carries great importance. That is because, among the various fishing rituals performed throughout Korea, the most important god is he who presides over the water itself—Yongwang. In the case of Shamanic faith, Yongwang oversees plentiful catches and has an intimate relationship to the spirits of those who drowned in the sea. *Yongwang-jae* is also carried out whenever there is a special occasion in a household. When someone is about to board a ship, someone is sick, or another important matter arises, these rituals are performed.

The rite is performed in the same space in each household—typically at the well inside the house or the communal village well. Sometimes, water will be brought from the village well into the kitchen of a home in a clay pot. Some rituals are conducted near the river, the mountains' springs, or the ocean. The water god is named either Sahae Yongwang (사해용왕, Yongwang of the Four Seas) or, by the mountainside, Sancheon Yongwang (산천용왕, Yongwang of Mountain Streams).

6. Obang Shinjang (오방신장, Five Direction Guardian God)

Obang Shinjang, Image from Sungje Cho's private collection

Shinjang refers to a god who plays the role of catching, trapping, or chasing away ghosts or other bad energies. A Taoist god in origin, Obang Shinjang is a mythological character and has influenced Korean indigenous faith and Shamanism. He is served as a guardian deity who traps or chases away a ghost that has entered a family home or village from any of the five directions: east, west, south, north, or center. While there are five gods responsible for each direction, they are collectively considered one divine deity and often portrayed in Shamanic paintings as five guardians.

The Shamanic tools included in this ritual, *Obangshinjang-gi* (오방신장기), are flags consisting of five colors (green, red, white, yellow, and black). After dancing with the five flags, the *mudang* makes the participant choose one of the flags without looking. This flag selection is then used to tell a fortune. The red flag is considered the best, and the black one is the worst. When the black flag is selected, the *mudang* performs cleansing rites to chase away dark energies and makes the participant select again, ensuring the selection of the red flag.

Another tool is *Shinjang-dae*, (신장대, Guardian God Stake). This is typically a bamboo stick attached to a scroll of white paper about

50 centimeters in length that is easy to grasp and shake. This tool is also used as a path of descent by the god and to chase away ghosts.

7. Dokkaebi (도깨비)

In Korean folktales, there are many stories related to *dokkaebi*. The amusing stories told to children at their grandmother's knees always included stories of *dokkaebi*. *Dokkaebi* gave blessings to kind people and punishments to those considered evil. It is said that when one makes a wish while tapping the *dokkaebi's* bat, everything wished will come true. For people forced into starvation and poverty, the idea that kindness will lead to a wish come true gave people hope and temporarily allowed them to forget life's anxieties. The *dokkaebi's* bat was an object desired by the working class and a subject of their longing.

Image from Seo Choi

Dokkaebi is an entirely different entity from other ghosts, which form after human beings die. It is believed that the materials used and tossed away in humans' everyday life, such as old brooms stained with blood, straw shoes, pokers, and old furniture, could transform into *dokkaebi*. At night, a fire of unknown cause, called *dokkaebi bul*, would light a flame in these objects and become *dokkaebi*. Another way in which *dokkaebi* are different from ghosts is that they don't only cause harm to human beings. Intensely mischievous, it is said that they also mislead and ridicule people, and when well-befriended, bring gold and silver treasures using supernatural powers and provide miraculous help.

The Korean *dokkaebi* is often drawn as comic and cute, while in Japan or China, *dokkaebi* are portrayed as frightful and monstrous. Given that it is all the same entity, one reason why China and Japan gave *dokkaebi* a horrible appearance is that their images may have originated from the 14th Hwan-Ung King, a direct ancestor of Korea, even before the time of *GoJoseon*.

The 14th Hwan-Ung King was also called Chiwoo Cheonwang (치우천왕) or *Dokkaebi* Emperor. His *dokkaebi* name originates from Chiwoo digging gunmetal and copper to make battle helmets modeled after a bull's head with two horns on each side. Because he was a great warrior, people saw him on the battlefield with a two-horned battle helmet and started calling him *dokkaebi*.

The *dokkaebi* who appears in Shamanism *Gut* is *Cheonshin Daegam geori* (천신대감거리). *Cheonshin Daegam* (천신대감) is called *Dokkaebi Daegam* and comes from Chiwoo, the 14th Hwan-Ung King. People believe that Chiwoo comes and goes from chimneys and fireplaces, leaving blessings and valuables. When the *mudang* plays *Cheonshin Daegam*, she performs the appearance of fireplace ash smeared on the face of the *dokkaebi*. Thus, it is said that the *mudang* brings good luck by spreading black ash on her hands and face and on the faces of others. In this way, *Cheonshin Daegam geori* is a fun *Gut*, leaving the *mudang* or members of the household performing the ritual clutching their bellies with laughter at the ridiculous appearance of the soot smears.

This performance also represents King Chiwoo's power over fire when he created bronze for the first time. Using his bronze sword and bull's-head helmet in war, Chiwoo always won the battles and seized control. Therefore Korea's *dokkaebi* became a deity in charge of chasing evil spirits out.

After his lifetime, civilians performed rites at Chiwoo's grave every fall, when it is said that one strand of red smoke would appear. From then on, the figure of *dokkaebi* was drawn as a red face with flaring eyes and a horned head. Later in China, dauntless and virtuous army generals came to color their faces red.

Among Shamanist *Guts*, there is one called *Gunwoonggeori* (군웅거리). This *Gut* recognizes the defeat of a ghost by the Chiwoo *Dokkaebi* Emperor. Some aristocratic homes and Buddhist temples would also bake roof slate tiles with the face of *dokkaebi* to deter evil spirits and ghosts. Even the totem poles at the entrance of villages, with two glaring eyes, were made to seek protection from any harm ghosts may bring. Their appearance is a modification of *dokkaebi's*.

On *Dano,* the fifth day of the fifth month of the lunar year, people make *Dano* charms and place them on the walls of their homes to chase away ghosts. In the ancient text of the Joseon dynasty, there is a phrase of protective talisman making: *'On May 5th, Dano, blessed by the heaven above and the earth below, and by the bronze head, steel forehead, red mouth and tongue of Chiwoo may immediately eliminate four hundred and four diseases.'*

This text shows the expectation that on *Dano,* when the heat of summer begins in earnest, Chiwoo will chase away all kinds of diseases that come with the heat. Certainly, it was believed that the *dokkaebi* could chase away capricious ghosts.

8. Seonghwang-shin and Seonang-shin (성황신, 서낭신, Village God)

Seonang-shin, Image from Sungje Cho's private collection

Seonghwang-shin and Seonang-shin are divinities that take different forms, but they both pray for the peace and happiness of the village. *Seonghwang-dang,* the shrines for Seonghwang, are centered primarily at the seaside, but *Seonang-dang* shrines are centered in the mountains and the inland region.

Seonghwang-shin refers to the village's guardian deity who prays for the village's peace and the development of each household. The village would build a shrine and place a deity, such as Sanshin, to be the guardian of the village.

The shrines were typically built and run by the state, but there were also occasions when rich and powerful countryside families would install them themselves. In these circumstances, the progenitor of the family or elders connected with the land were received as the deity.

In the early Joseon dynasty, altars were combined and rearranged into a single shrine for Sunghwang. In the spring and fall, the chief carried out rites regularly. The ritual was also carried out during times of national crisis and drought. As it was incorporated into the institution of the state, the various levels of the altar became fixed, and the scale of *Seonghwang-dang* (Shrine for Seonghwang), the ceremony, and the size and shape of the deity were prescribed in detail. In the designated *Seonghwang-dang*, a manager was appointed, and he was released from taxation and military services.

All over Korea, it is possible to find shrines and sacred trees devoted to Seonghwang-shin. While some records say that Seonghwang-shin began in China and crossed over to the Korean Peninsula, Seonghwang-shin is, in fact, a deity indigenous to our clan and comes from *Sodo*, a rite offered to the heavenly spirit during the period of *Budoji*. Likely, rituals to Seonghwang-shin were first devoted to the gods of wind, clouds, thunder, and rain, related to agriculture, to wish for a year of good harvest.

On the other hand, Seonang-shin is a divinity that is a fusion of a tree god and a mountain god. It originates from the ancient *Sodo* of *Budoji* to protect the village from harm, disease, disaster, and calamity and to resolve the fundamental problems of human livelihood. Usually, a pile of broken stones is placed before a divine tree, or at the summit of a hill where the tree is attached to the *mudang*'s house, on the side of the road, at the village entrance, or at the entrance of a Buddhist temple. Many of these trees have been cut down through modernization and development or destroyed as a sign of devilish worship by Westernized religions that later entered Korea.

Seonang-shin also keeps travelers safe and protects them from encountering evil spirits and other harm on the road. On the first full moon of the lunar new year, people pray that he will extinguish hardship and calamity and bring blessings. They present offerings that can be found on the side of roads and in various nooks and crannies around a village.

The altar for Seonang-shin consists of a stack of small stones, and passersby are invited to add to the mound as they desire. These altars of stacked stone are also found at the foot of trees and, sometimes, beside shrines for Sanshin.

At the *Seonang-dang*, the shrine, the branches of the tree contain countless pieces of cotton cloth, mulberry paper, five-colored silks, clothing, hair, bowls of blood, money, and other offerings. The money is hung to win profits in business, the pieces of cotton cloth to pray for a child's long life, and the five-colored silk is hung to protect a newlywed bride and groom.

Women occasionally leave an offering of rice at the stone altar by the tree and pray for the well-being or healing of sick children. Then, after their prayer, they feed the ill child the rice offering. Other times, Korean shamans are paid to perform rites for the parents.

Passersby can perform a simple custom for a safe journey: throwing a small piece of rock over the stone altar or spitting in that direction. Spitting like this is a way to escape any evil spirits floating around.

9. Goonwoong-shin (군웅신, Warrior/Hero God)

Goonwoong-shin is a Shamanic warrior god. Originally, *goonwoong* referred to an exceptionally-skilled king revered as a hero. The exact origin is unclear, but it is said that ancient Korea's 14th Hwang-Ung King Chiwoo became the first Goonwoong-shin after his death.

Over the centuries, Goonwoong-shin was said to have an excellent ability to chase away or extinguish evil spirits and demons. But presently, Goonwoong-shin is considered a warrior or hero deity of Korean Shamanism.

Shamanic Warrior God and Goddess, Image from Sungje Cho's private collection

10. Okhwang Sangjae (옥황상제, Celestial Emperor God)

Okhwang Sangjae occupies the highest level of divinity among those that rule the heavens. Originally, Okhwang Sangjae was worshipped in popular Taoism in China and transmitted to Korea, where he was received as a Shamanic god. Traditionally in Korea, he is understood as the divinity supervising heaven and is identified as the Source, the God Almighty.

Okhwang Sangje, Image from Sungje Cho's private collection

Okhwang Sangjae is deemed essential for humans' everyday life, blessing them with long and healthy lives or good or bad luck. In the painting of Shamanic Deities, Okhwang Sangjae is portrayed as a grandfather wearing a yellow, red, or white color robe with a crown, a long white beard, and his hands holding a scepter at his chest.

In Shamanic belief, Okhwang Sangjae is considered the most extraordinary god. Still, as one entity among many gods, he does not have a massive influence over the work of the shamans. However, all Korean shamans have in common the practice of worshipping him as the supreme deity. The heaven where Okhwang Sangjae resides is called *Jamiwon* (자미원), and his palace is called *Jamigung* (자미궁).

5) SIGNIFICANCE OF RITUAL TOOLS

Korean *mudang*s use a variety of Shamanic tools in *Gut* or divination. There are three types of tools that are the most representative of the Shamanic tools used to appeal to and commune with gods: *myeongdu* (명두, a sacred mirror), a Shamanic rattle (방울), and a fan (부채).

1. *Myeongdu,* Sacred Mirror: How Gods Descend

All Korean *mudang* have one or two *myeongdu*, also sometimes called a sacred mirror or copper mirror. *Mudang*s regard *myeongdu* as much more precious than other tools and handle them with utmost care. Older female shamans tend to collect many and often leave behind their own *myeongdu* for the shamans who follow their work.

Myeongdu is commonly used far and wide by shamans across East Asia. In Korea's Hwanghae province, there was an old saying that *mudang*s carry mirrors on their chest when they perform *Gut*. When performing *Gut* on ships, they would hang *myeongdu* on the sails.

In Siberia, shamans have robes decorated with the sun, moon, and stars, and shamans of Mongolia would hang their sacred mirrors in their shrines or perform rituals carrying the mirror on their chest. They would embroider the sun, moon, and stars in their ritual garments.

The *myeongdu* of China are a little different from that of Korea. The mirror's backside bears the sun and moon, but it doesn't have the Big Dipper or the stars like Korea's. The uses of *myeongdu* in Japan are as varied as in Korea. Many shrines in Japan hang the sacred mirror next to offerings of paper streamers. Their *myeongdu* also lack celestial patterns.

Typically, *myeongdu* is made from brass and the front bulges like the lid of a rice bowl. It is shiny, with a rough, concave backside.

As the name indicates—*myeong* meaning light, and *du* meaning mirror—it should always have a pattern of the sun, moon, and the seven stars of the Big Dipper. While some scholars say that there are categories of *myeongdu* without the celestial elements, *myeongdu* that do not bear the sun, moon, and Big Dipper cannot be considered a proper *myeongdu*.

The *myeongdu* is displayed by connecting a tri-colored (red, green, and yellow) fabric on the shrine's wall and then hanging it above the fabric. Different shamans hang the mirror on the various deities they serve. The intent of all the gods can be delivered through *myeongdu*.

A very small *myeongdu* can be attached to the Shamanic rattle and used to communicate with the gods or to chase away evil spirits. One must fold a white mulberry paper and cover the mirror when hanging it. When a shaman stands a *myeongdu* along the Shamanic fan placed next to the altar, the mirror represents the deity the shaman is serving.

Among many different types of *myeongdu*, the celestial one with patterns of sun, moon, and stars is most treasured by the *mudangs*. That is because when initiated through the *Naerim* ritual, they received their gods through the celestial *myeongdu* hanging on top of a celestial stake, a Shamanic tool of about one meter, used to receive and greet the gods of the sun, moon, and stars. The *myeongdu* hung from the stake plays an antenna-like role, facilitating communication between the gods and the person receiving them. Since this ritual is how *mudangs* first experienced communion with the gods, the celestial *myeongdu* is treasured.

Celestial Stake & *Myeongdu* placed together to invoke a goddess deity

Usually, pine trees are used for this celestial stake (일월대) because shamans believed pine and bamboo had cleansing power. Only pine branches stretching towards the east could be cut down for use, a length just less than a meter. The pine branches were cut into a shape resembling a human body, with a torso, limbs, and head. Then, the branches were dressed to reflect the deities. This custom of dressing sacred branches or trees, originating from the time of Ancient Joseon of the *Budoji* period, continues today.

While *myeongdu* is a Shamanic divination tool for communicating with gods, it can also represent the Supreme God. As a symbol of absolute power, its reflective brilliance can't be looked at directly by anyone when illuminated by sunlight. This indicates its symbolism of an absolute god, displaying the might of the omnipotent being whom nobody dares overlook. Similarly, at night, when the *myeongdu* reflects the moonlight and is charged with the energy of the Big Dipper, its light emits benevolence, delicateness, and tenderness, creating the appearance of divine mystery distinct from that of an absolute god.

Thus, when the *myeongdu* reflects the sun, moon, and Big Dipper, the *myeongdu* itself becomes the universe. The moment it is hung, the vast universe is transferred to the mirror. When *mudang*s sit in their shrines and pray through *myeongdu*, they communicate with universal wavelengths and energy and progress towards embracing the heart of the universe.

2. Rattles: Calling To and Invoking Gods

Among the Shamanic tools used by a *mudang*, one is indispensable: the rattle. Rattles are an essential symbol of Korean shamans.

Typically, when one thinks of a bell or rattle, one may picture the small clapper inside a bell that creates sound, but Shamanic bells are slightly different. With the Shamanic instrument, many brass bells are struck against one another, producing a sound.

Korean shamans utilize both bells and rattles in their practice, using clear metallic sounds to invoke spirits and communicate with them, and these sounds can ward off evil spirits. The bells are typically hung at the shrine and played in the morning and evening during prayer or blessings.

The Shamanic rattles are sometimes used to test the ability and power of the *mudang* during their initiation ritual. Many *mudang*s use the rattles to provide psychic readings, divination, or perform an exorcism.

Usually, white, red, yellow, and sometimes navy pieces of cloth are hung from the end of the rattle. It's difficult to guess when and where this tradition began, but it likely has indigenous origins, from distant ancestors performing rituals to heaven while holding on to a white ox's tail.

Below are descriptions of different types of Shamanic rattles.

Daeshin Rattle (대신방울) is typically used by *mudang* when providing psychic readings or divination. There are four brass stakes with three bells each, so the twelve bells are used to make sounds. This type of rattle is most commonly used by shamans in the Seoul area.

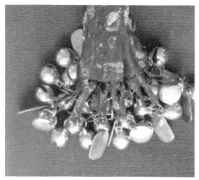

Ninety-nine Rattle

Ninety-nine Rattle (아흔아홉상쇠방울) is the rattle of the *mudang*s from Hwanghae province. Consisting of 99 tiny bells, it is also called a *sangswae* bell. Out of the 99 bells, several specially shaped bells have a particular purpose. Some are inscribed with "life" and "blessing" to help people's well-being. Some are shaped like the sacred mirror *myeongdu* to assist in connection and communication with the gods. There are also bells called "gateway" to represent the path via which gods are received and bells representing yin and yang, or duality and balance. A few rattles are larger and shaped angularly differently to simulate *dokkaebi*, used to drive out evil spirits. One bell is rough in texture for use with rice grains in divination. Many other bells reflect different purposes, such as good health, healing, fortune, and more.

Chilsung **Rattle** (칠성방울, Seven Star Rattle) consists of seven bells and is used during the *Chilsung* ritual to aid in long life and blessings. The *mudang*s who use this rattle are steadily disappearing today.

Goonwoong **Rattle** (군웅방울) is used during the *Goonwoong* ritual and is usually hung on the end of a wooden stake. The *mudang* creates a wrap from the clothing of families who requested the ritual, then drapes a piece of white hemp cloth and hangs the rattle on top. This seems to have originated with ancient Hwan-Ung King Chiwoo, also called Great *Dokkaebi* King. After his death, people memorialized him with a flag of *dokkaebi* on a stake to honor his powers, so this custom may come from that ancient tradition of asking Chiwoo's power to ward off evil spirits and energies.

These rattles were the most essential Shamanic tools to *mudang*s and fundamental symbols to ancient kings. In ancient Korea, those in leadership roles included a king and a shaman priest, and the rattles and other evidence of their dual role have been found in old archeological sites and referenced in ancient texts.

3. Shamanic Fan: Recalling the Teachings of Samshin

As an indispensable Shamanic tool, the types of fans used by *mudang*s vary. While every *mudang* uses it differently, before a *Gut* begins, they hold the fan in their right hand and the rattle in their left to summon the gods. The rattle communes with the gods via sound waves, and the fan invokes the gods via wind waves. The *Chilsung* fan causes the wind to invoke the Chilsungshin, while the Daeshin fan causes the wind to invoke the Daeshin goddess. According to the *Budoji*, Mago appeared—or was born from—*YulYeo*, the sounds and vibration of the universe, caused and disseminated by the wind.

Here emerges the reason *mudang*s use rattles and fans simultaneously when appealing to the gods. Through sound and vibration, rattles give birth to *YulYeo*, while fans cause wind and, through airwaves, resemble *YulYeo* and facilitate communication with the gods.

When *mudang*s carry out *Gut*, they tie either a white or three-colored fabric to their fans. On *Chilsung* fans, they tie a long piece of white fabric to represent a rare sacred white snake. This was because the ancestors believed the shape of a serpent resembled the Big Dipper constellation (*Chilsung*) and often used the snake as a sacred totem. When *mudang*s hung tricolored fabric to their fans, it represented the three divine markers of heaven, earth, and humanity and Mago Samshin, the Triple Goddess.

Shamanic dancing is an activity that reenacts the sound and vibration

AN OVERVIEW OF KOREAN SHAMANISM

of the eight notes of sound, *YulYeo*—the divine wisdom and direct teachings of Mago Samshin. To reenact the sound of *YulYeo*, a wind must be generated. This can be done by dancing and making large bodily movements while holding the fan. Even today, *mudangs* shake their fan as they dance. The fans and rattles *mudangs* use while performing *Gut* establish the Korean people's original identity as descendants of the indigenous clan created by Mago Samshin.

Other musical instruments that are indispensable to *Gut* are drums and gongs. Gongs are said to make the sound of the earth, and drums are the sound of the heavens. Thus, to beat drums and gongs is to recreate the sound of the universe: *YulYeo*, the harmony. *YulYeo*, the universal vibrational harmony of heaven and earth, edifies humans to recover their true nature.

Daeshin (Mudang Goddess), shown with the *myeongdu*, fan, and the rattle. Image from Sungje Cho's private collection

6) THE SHAMANIC MEANING OF THE CROSS

The cross is an emblem of Christianity, deemed absolute and held sacred by Christians. Representing Jesus, the cross is also believed to exhibit holy power when warding off demons.

Nowadays, crosses are worn by many as accessories: necklaces, rings, and earrings. This originates in the psychology of seeking to ward off evil ghosts through the energy held by a sacred object.

In Korean Shamanism, gods whose role is to chase away ghosts or evil spirits are called Shinjang (신장). The cross appears as a symbol of Shinjang.

The origins of the Shamanic cross can be found in ancient Korean astronomy. In the East, constellations are categorized by three celestial regions. The North Star, said to determine the growth and extinction of all things, is at the center, considered the palace of the heavens. *Jamigung*, the palace, is protected by twenty-eight stars. These twenty-eight stars are distributed in sets of seven in the east, west, south, and north. In Korean Shamanism, these stars oversee the role of the deity Shinjang, chasing away and trapping evil spirits and ghosts. The constellation that represents these twenty-eight stars is a cross.

When *mudang*s carry out *Gut*, they often make a gesture of crossing two Shamanic tools, like ceremonial swords, because the shape of the cross represents the defeat of evil energy. It is also believed that if the blades are thrown outward, they must land crossing each other to ensure the ghost has departed effectively. The ceremony can only end after the shaman picks up the thrown swords and makes a cross shape with them on the ground.

Another sign of the cross is in the power of creation itself. In Chinese characters, the number ten is the shape of a cross. As mentioned earlier, the cross carries the meaning of the creation of heaven and earth. But the actual creation of heaven and earth is not the cross of Christianity, the cross drawn by *mudang*s on the ground, or the cross used on certain talismans, but the reproductive organs of women: the tenth hole. Now considered an insult used against women, the *shipgumeong* (십구멍, the tenth hole) represents the womb, the gate of creation. It is women's "ten" in the shape of a cross that creates heaven and earth with the birth of new life.

According to *Budoji*, humanity began with Mago and her two daughters, Gung-hee and So-hee. When *Budoji* says that Mago and her two daughters created heaven and earth, it is saying that the person who possesses the ability to create life is a woman; thus, humanity's start is due to womankind. It is not excessive imagining to think that Samshin Halmoni, a woman who possesses the 'ten,' the womb, is the ultimate god who created the universe.

Furthermore, the creation of new life requires ten months of residing in a mother's womb upon conception. Why ten months? Because to open the four directions and come out, the number ten must be filled. The true cross signifies the womb of woman, the creator of new life, which both conceals and bears the wisdom of the universe.

7) THE SHAMANIC VIEW OF DEATH AND THE AFTERLIFE

1. The Shamanic Understanding of Death

Since long ago, the Shamanic faith has grown naturally, passed down as a folk belief among ordinary people. Because of this, it does not have a specified doctrine, system, or religious order and has maintained a Shamanist form of spirituality. Just as the Shamanic practices vary by region, their rituals of death vary by region also.

In Korean culture, death can be summarized as a return. When someone dies, it is said they "returned." While there is no clear answer as to where they return, possibilities can be surmised through observing the traditional funeral ceremony.

After death, the corpse is carried out on a board called *chilsung-pan* (칠성판, Seven Star Board), with seven holes in the shape of the Big Dipper. The corpse and board are then wrapped in white cloth and laid inside the coffin. This rite suggests that when someone died, it was believed their soul returned to the Big Dipper. In the Shamanic faith, the Big Dipper is worshipped as the Chilsungshin (칠성신) who presides over humans' life, health, and fortunes.

There are atypical deaths, for instance, those who die at a young age, in roadside accidents, deaths caused by violent acts, or other unnatural causes. On these occasions, the souls of the dead become unable to go to the next world and linger in mid-heaven, sometimes called limbo, imposing harm on the living. Conversely, there are deaths from natural causes, which are accepted without any doubt.

The deceased person who died a normal death takes their place as a harmless, traditional ancestor, but those who suffer unusual deaths cannot become ancestors and are thought to devolve into ghosts. The funeral ceremony procedures for each of these deaths are different, and people's attitudes toward each kind of death are also different.

Unnatural deaths may cause souls to become dangerous spiritual entities capable of causing harm to their descendants while aimlessly wandering about this world, unable to wholly enter the otherworld. Thus, the Shamanic ritual of safely sending these souls to the otherworld by appeasing and comforting them so they do not hurt their descendants emerged as *Gut* itself.

In Korean Shamanism, it is believed there are benevolent spirits as well as evil spirits. Evil spirits may bring death to humans by infecting them with disease. The disease is cured if the benevolent spirit can ward off the evil one. If the evil spirit wins, the person dies.

In Korean Shamanism, dying after completing one's so-called divine fate is ideal. It is thought that to live a long and healthy life is the greatest ideal. It is believed that to suffer the misfortune of death at a young age, before having completed one's fate, would accumulate more *han*[53] (한), and unfortunate deaths are created by the meddling of an evil spirit.

In Korean Shamanism, the most essential practice is alleviating or neutralizing the dead's *han* after death. The thought is that it is necessary

---

53) *Han* (한) is a uniquely Korean term of burden in body and soul. While there is no completely accurate English translation, *han* can be described as an internalized feeling that blends deep sorrow, resentment, grief, regret, and anger.

to offer consolation regarding an unfair death; when one dies, not every-thing disappears but the deceased leaves a trace in the world of the living. Ordinarily, people may believe one's ties to the human world are cut off at death. But in Korean Shamanism, one's relationship to the human world, especially to their descendants, is not easily severed but persists for a long time.

A deceased person's soul maintains relationships with the living. It is believed that these relations emerge from unfortunate deaths more than benign ones. A spirit who suffered a regrettable death may torture people persistently until the deceased's resentment is fully resolved. In this situa-tion, it is believed that the deceased's resentment must be solved through a Shamanic ceremony. Shamanic rites can relieve the deceased who feel victimized by their death and have lots of bitterness about their lives.

The Shamanic ritual of *Gut* is carried out to prevent evil influence. Even if the deceased person, as a hostile entity, carries *han*, it is believed that if their *han* is resolved, they will change into a benevolent ancestor who offers blessings to humans.

Through the Shamanic ritual of *Gut*, it is possible to remove the neg-ative element rupturing a soul's relationship with the living, breaking the emotional wall, and facilitating peace and divine reincarnation.

Funeral ceremony methods vary globally and are informed mainly by the geographic environment. Fundamental differences arise from each regional group's view of death, which cannot help but influence its approach to the form and procedures of a funeral service. Different religions offer answers to individual questions about life and death, but styles of explanation are not based on a medical or scientific doctrine but are somewhat subjective.

Through funeral rites and methods demanded by the constituents of society, humans can discover how they think about and accept death. As they learn how to satisfy the methods demanded by society, they find the socially required attitude toward death. The rite of passage of another's death becomes an occasion for examining one's own life and contemplating how humans can live meaningful lives. Managing a deceased person's corpse takes on a more significant meaning and forms the views on death in that region or ethnic group. Thus, the culture of funeral ceremonies and death's rites of passage include a complex entanglement with attitudes toward understanding death.

2. The View of the Afterlife in Korean Shamanism

Perspectives on the afterlife center around the soul, specifically where it goes and in what form it exists after a human dies. All understandings of the afterlife are rooted in the soul's emotional state and how living descendants think of the soul. If the soul does not exist, there cannot be an understanding of the afterlife; therefore, *Gut* cannot exist. Thus, believing in the soul's immortality forms the core view of the afterlife.

Afterlife answers the question of whether or not one will continue existing after death. Will life continue even after the end of life? Such a question is self-contradictory, but all religions speak of the existence of life after death, signifying the universally-held belief that a completely different "consciousness"—the soul—continues to exist after physical death. In other words, a human consists of the physical body and the soul; these two elements belong to entirely different dimensions.

In this way, the afterlife, where the soul will live after one dies (Shamanist afterlife,) is a horizontal, two-dimensional world of experience that extends from the human world. This understanding of the afterlife as similar to bodily life reflects Shamanist realism. It is not that the deceased become extinct but remains in soul form, residing where all souls linger.

The afterlife is where thoughts, awareness, and character are settled. Because of this, even when the physical body is extinguished, one's existence can continue. From a metaphysical perspective, this immaterial existence is called the soul. This notion of the world where souls live after death, the world where the souls of ancestors reside, appears in Shamanism as simply the "good place." This is a place of peace, abundance, and comfort, free of suffering and conflicts.

Unlike other religions that proclaim salvation, the Shamanic afterlife is part of a natural cycle without a sense of redemption, dissimilar from heaven or hell. What used to be part of the cycle of a soul's journey was eventually modified through the influence of Buddhism, influenced by the Buddhist view of death, the afterlife, and the existence of heaven and hell.

While the Shamanic notion of a "heaven and hell" was influenced by Buddhist philosophy, some also argue that the elements of Korean Shamanism were incorporated into Korean Buddhism. *Cheondoje* (천도제), the Korean Buddhist death rites, are a combination of Korean Shamanistic and original Buddhist death rites from India.

In Korean Shamanism, the afterlife is often described as a paradise, similar to the Buddhist Elysium. In this paradise, flowers bloom in all four seasons, and human souls are free of suffering, experiencing happiness without fear of death. Meanwhile, hell is described as terrible—a very difficult, dangerous, painful place the soul must travel through to arrive at paradise, with their ultimate goal/destination being reincarnation.

There are a variety of states of hell: one of knife blades, one of fire, one of poisonous snakes, one of freezing ice, one of pitch-black darkness, and others. These different hells appear in the Shamanic songs of *Jinogi Gut* (death rituals) as difficult milestones the deceased must cross on their journey to the otherworld.

According to Shamanic storytelling songs, the deceased's journey through these difficult obstacles can be assisted by good deeds and relationships they build while living. In some of these stories, the assistance shows up as people who have died earlier, appearing in spirit form and capable of providing superhuman or magical powers not affected by the time and space constraints of the human world. This speaks to the idea that whether living or deceased, the lives of souls cannot be lived alone. While alive, one must be generous to many friends and act with kindness, and in this way, the journey to the afterlife is not notably different from one's lifetime.

Ultimately, the view of the afterlife in Korean Shamanism can be summarized into the following categories.

1. *Haewon Sungsaeng* (해원성생) — Alleviating *Han* and Making Rebirth Available

The neutralization of *han* caused by the manner of death holds the greatest importance. This includes the idea that when someone dies, they leave something behind in the world of the living rather than disappear without a trace. It is thought that upon death, one does not easily cut off ties with human society but maintains persistent relations. If the resentment of the deceased is not entirely resolved, negative energy is directed toward the bereaved. The soul of those who died unfairly, carrying resentment, have greater influence than those who died having lived with kindness. This kind of death, in which a ghost cannot go to the afterlife and roams the world imposing harm to family or others, holds the greatest importance in the Shamanic view of death. This kind of death can only achieve a peaceful rebirth for the deceased with an appropriate Shamanic ceremony.

2. Heaven and Hell in Korean Shamanistic Views

In Korean Shamanism, the world is divided into heaven (the sky) and earth (the land). The heavenly world (where souls go in the afterlife) is where immortals (deities and gods) live, and it is the same place as the paradise referred in Buddhism. It is a place of happiness where beautiful flowers bloom year-round, free of suffering, resentment, or death. On the other hand, the land, the earth, and the human world are places where those who committed sins in the heavens are sometimes exiled. The difficult and painful nature of human life itself is considered a punishment for sins made in the heavens. There are several Shamanic songs about immortals fulfilling their karma in the human world to be forgiven of their sins to ascend to heaven.

3. Karma, or Retributive Justice

Suffering due to wrongdoing in a past life is a form of retribution. And those who committed wrongdoing must pay out the cost of their sin before being allowed entrance into paradise and eventual reincarnation. One can enter paradise and enjoy comfort after death by committing plentiful good deeds and acting with kindness and generosity while living.

4. Grace and Expressing Gratitude

When the deceased receive assistance from ancestor spirits to safely overcome their journey in the afterlife, they often express thanks to their helper spirits with incense or offerings. Just as in folktales of the human world, Shamanic stories and myths stress that in the journey to the afterlife, one must deliver thanks to those who offered help. Expressing grace and gratitude is a person's duty, whether toward a living being, ghost, or god.

5. A Universal View of Life

According to this view, one's life in the human world determines what kind of treatment one will receive in the afterlife. It was thought that the afterlife was typically determined according to the gods' intentions. Death was considered an uncontrollable event malleable to the decisions of the gods, where they chose humans to die or live, depending on their needs for the humans' service.

6. The Ideology of Reincarnation in Paradise as Influenced by Buddhism

The basic Shamanic view of the afterlife—the idea of the "good place"—was influenced by Buddhism to include a basic understanding of heaven and hell. This included the idea that when one does many good deeds in life, they will live comfortably in an eternity of paradise. When they commit evil acts, they descend to hell and receive retribution is an ideology that is now spread widely in Shamanism.

7. Ideas of Rebirth & Reincarnation

When one dies, one is eventually reborn again in the human world. Once one's time in the afterlife is served, they are returned to the human world as a human or animal. People wish to be born again as humans rather than animals, hoping for better circumstances than their present ones—a better home, the only heir in a wealthy household, someone of higher class or improved rank. Thus, integral in the Shamanic view of the afterlife is the idea that subsequent lives are always preferable to present ones.

APPENDIX 5
Myth of Jesang Park

In the year 390, the king of ancient Japan sent a diplomat to the king of Silla, King Naemul.

"Our king has great respect for your divine abilities and asks that you send one of your princes to Japan as a sign of gratitude," the diplomat said. So King Naemul sent his third son, Mihae, who was just 10 years old. The Japanese king kept Mihae hostage for 30 years.

Then, in the year 419, three years after his oldest son took the throne as King Nulji, the king of Goguryeo sent a diplomat to Silla with the message, "Our king has heard your younger brother, Bohae, is bright and talented. He would like to build a friendship with Silla. Please send your brother to visit, as emissary." King Nulji heard this and felt it a good diplomatic move, so he sent his younger brother to Goguryeo. This time, the king of Goguryeo kept Bohae hostage and did not return him.

In the year 425, King Nulji invited his officials, heroes, and warriors to the palace, where he hosted a party featuring a feast and musicians. After three rounds of rice wine and other alcohol, music began to play. Listening, the king teared up, telling his officials, "While my father ruled with good intentions, thinking only of his own people, he sent his dear son to Japan in a gesture of gratitude and never saw him again. He passed into death without ever reuniting."

King Nulji continued, "Then when I became king, the neighboring country of Goguryeo had such a strong military who never stopped warring with us that when they sent word seeking our friendship I trusted their word and sent my younger brother to Goguryeo. They, too, kept my brother hostage and haven't returned him. Oh, what I wouldn't give to see both brothers again! Together, we could perform ancestral rituals at my father's altar. This would be such a blessing!"

Gazing at his officials, he questioned, "I wonder who can make this happen?"

The officials said, "Certainly, this is not an easy task. We need someone with intelligence, cleverness, and courage. Only someone with such attributes could make your hopes possible."

After some thought, the officials spoke again. "We believe that the local official of Sabra province, Park Jesang, is the right choice."

So the king called Jesang into his quarters and made his request. After bowing twice, Jesang answered, "I have heard that if a king has worries, then it causes strife for those who serve him. If the king is disrespected or shamed, then those who serve him must die. If I first measured whether the task you have presented me with is difficult or easy, before making my commitment, then I would be neither a brave nor loyal servant. If I first think about whether I'll live or die before deciding to take action, then I will have made my decision without courage."

Park Jesang paused before speaking again. "Although I do not consider myself worthy enough, I would like to honor your wishes and return your brothers to you." King Nulji felt moved by Jesang's words and poured him rice wine. Together they drank, and King Nulji clasped Jesang's hands when saying goodbye.

Jesang immediately went to Goguryeo as an emissary, meeting Prince Bohae to discuss his escape. On May 15, as they planned, he waited for the prince at the Gosung pier. As part of their plot, the prince feigned illness for a few days prior, remaining inactive in his quarters. That night, he escaped to the beach. When the King of Goguryeo discovered his absence, he sent many soldiers to capture Bohae once again. However, the prince had been kind and generous to the soldiers while living as a hostage, so the soldiers pitied him, sparing him by shooting arrows without heads. In this way, Prince Bohae was able to return to Silla unharmed.

When King Nulji saw his brother Bohae again, the thought of his other brother Mihae arose as well, making their reunion a bittersweet one. With tears in his eyes, King Nulji said, "It is as if I have a body with only one arm and one eye. Whilst I have regained one, I still don't have the other, and this saddens me."

Once Jesang heard this he left the palace once again, not even returning home to see his own family before embarking upon his second quest. Instead, he went straight to the pier of Yulpo in order to leave for Japan, to retrieve the second prince. When Jesang's wife heard this, she ran out of their house and followed him on horseback. However, her husband was already on the boat when she arrived at the pier. She cried and called his name sadly, yet her husband only waved at her as the boat set sail for Japan.

Jesang arrived in Japan, announcing to Japan's king, "The king of Silla killed my father and brothers, who were innocent of any crime, so I have come here to seek refuge." It was a cunning plot and the king of Japan believed him, offering Jesang a house to live in comfortably. Living there, Jesang often accompanied Prince Mihae to the beach to hunt birds and fish. Each time he caught anything good, he made an offering of his catch to the Japanese king. The king enjoyed these offerings and never doubted Jesang's loyalty.

One day, when the early morning fog was so thick that one could not even see their hands held in front of their face, Park Jesang told Prince Mihae, "Now you are ready to leave."

"Then let us go together," Prince Mihae said.

But Jesang replied, "If I go with you, the Japanese will know of our plot and follow us. I wish to stay here, preventing suspicion and delaying their pursuit of you."

"You have become like a father and an older brother to me. How could I leave you and return alone?" the prince replied.

Jesang said, "If I could save your life to appease King Nulji and heal a brother's heart, then that is enough for me. How could I wish for anything more in my life?" Then, Jesang poured wine for Prince Mihae, sending him off to his escape, accompanied by another official of Silla. Then, Park Jesang waited inside Prince Mihae's room, to see what would unfold.

The next morning, Japanese officials arrived to visit Prince Mihae. They were greeted by Park Jesang instead, who prevented them from entering Prince Mihae's room, saying, "Yesterday the prince did so much hunting and running around, he is too exhausted to get up and host visitors." In the afternoon, the officials grew curious and asked again. Then, Jesang replied, "The prince left a long time ago."

The officials ran to tell the king of Japan, who sent soldiers on horseback to chase after Prince Mihae, but they were not able to catch him.

The king of Japan imprisoned Park Jesang, asking, "Why did you secretly return the prince to his homeland?"

Jesang said, "I am a servant of Silla, not a servant of Japan. I only meant to follow my king's order. I have nothing more to say to you."

This angered the king of Japan, who said, "You were already acting as my servant, and now you betray me by saying you are still a servant of Silla. You will be harshly punished unless you admit that you will now live as a servant of Japan. If you swear your loyalty to me, I will reward you with a position and prize."

But Park Jesang replied, "I would rather be a dog or a pig of Silla than become a servant of Japan. I would take the harshest punishment in Silla before accepting a position and a salary from Japan."

The angry king then ordered the bottom of Jesang's feet to be stripped of skin, making him walk on the sharp edges of cut reeds. He then asked again, "Whose servant are you?"

Jesang replied, "I am a servant of Silla!"

Furious, the king of Japan then stood Jesang on top of a burning hot iron and asked, "Whose servant are you?"

Jesang replied, "I am a servant of Silla!"

At this, the king realized he could not break Jesang, and burned him to death on the island of Mokdo.

When Prince Mihae returned to Silla, King Nulji and his brother Bohae received him at the pier. The three brothers returned to the palace to hold a feast in celebration, and King Nulji ordered a broad pardon across the nation, to celebrate. He gave Park Jesang's wife the title of The Great Mother of the Nation and arranged for Jesang's daughter to marry Prince Mihae.

When Park Jesang's wife heard the news of his leaving for Japan, without first returning home, she stood at the edge of the sea and wailed with sadness for her husband for a long time. After this, people renamed the beach The Never-Ending Cry Beach. Even long after her husband's death, Park Jesang's wife often climbed to the top of Chisulryeong Mountain with her two daughters, to weep in the direction of Japan. It is said that she died on that mountain top, still and crying, and turned into a stone.

The stone remained at the top of Chisulryeong Mountain, deified as sacred, and Park Jesang's wife was deified as the guardian spirit of Mount Chisulryeong. A shrine was built there to honor her as well, as ChisulShinmo, the Mother Spirit of Mount Chisul.

Translator's Note: This story was translated from a chapter in the ancient text, *Sauguk Yusa*. The shrine for Park Jesang's wife may have still been intact at the time *Samguk Yusa* was published in 1281 CE, but the shrine no longer exists in modern Korea. However, the sacred stone still remains. Today, visitors and tourists to the area will find a new memorial built to honor Park Jesang and his family.

the
CREATIVE
TEAM

INTERPRETATION BY SUNGJE CHO

 Sungje Cho (조성제) was born in Daegu. He is an author, scholar, and educator. He received a doctorate in Korean Folklore with specialty in Korean Shamanism from Dongbang Culture University and teaches courses related to Korean Shamanism. He served as an editor-in-chief of the World Shamanism Newspaper and is a member of various organizations such as Korean Shamanism Research Council and Association of Ancient East Asian Researchers. He is an author of many books in Korea, including *Stories of Korean Shamanism inside Indigenous Culture, Mudang, Overview of Korean Shamanism,* and *Gods and Gut Rituals of Korean Shamanism.* Sungje wrote the commentary as well as the Overview of Korean Shamanism in this publication, *Budoji: A Tale of the Divine City of Ancient Korea.*

ORIGINAL TEXT BY JESANG PARK

Budoji was written by a loyal Silla official named Jesang Park (박제상, 363–419 CE). It was a chapter in a larger collection of books called *Jing Shim Rok,* which was passed down through his family over the generations. It was later introduced to the world in 1953 by one of his descendants, who was also a journalist.

There is a myth about Park's loyalty to the Silla king and his wife's love for him in *Samguk Yusa.* The English translation by Seo Choi is shared in this book in the Appendix.

TRANSLATION, EDITING, PUBLISHING BY SEO CHOI

Seo Choi (최서희) was born in Seoul and immigrated to the United States in 1991. She is a Korean American shaman, author, and the founder of Alpha Sisters Publishing. She is the creator of the Morning Calm Oracle, an oracle deck influenced by Korean ancestry, and the author of *Don't Be a B*tch, Be an Alpha*. Seo has translated, edited, and published a photo essay book by Chanho Park, *Return: Korea's Rituals of Death, Spirits, and Ancestors*. She is based in Atlanta, GA.

ILLUSTRATION BY MEESHA GOLDBERG

Meesha Goldberg was born in Queens, NY and is a Korean American artist, poet, and gardener living in Virginia. Her primary medium is oil paint, which she uses to render realistic, mystical landscapes that speak to humanity's belonging and responsibility to the Earth. Goldberg has exhibited in galleries across the country with solo shows in Portland, Los Angeles, Seattle, and most recently at Second Street Gallery in Charlottesville with her installation "Daughterland."

Made in the USA
Coppell, TX
20 December 2023

26661471R00098